P9-CEM-703

Tea Celebrations

Also by Alexandra Stoddard

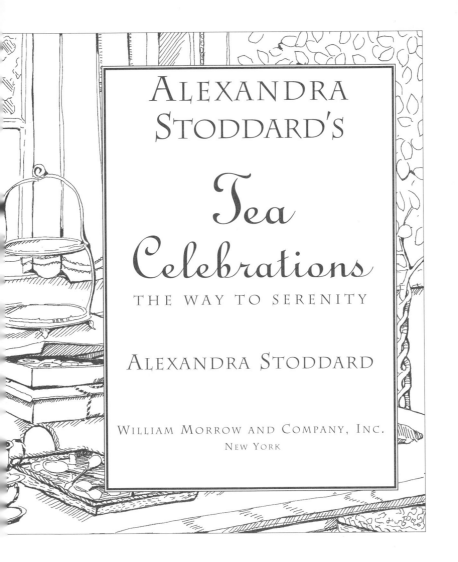

ALEXANDRA STODDARD'S

Tea Celebrations

THE WAY TO SERENITY

ALEXANDRA STODDARD

WILLIAM MORROW AND COMPANY, INC.
NEW YORK

It is the policy of William Morrow and Company, Inc.,
and its imprints and affiliates, recognizing the importance of
preserving what has been written, to print the books we publish
on acid-free paper, and we exert our best efforts to that end.

Library of Congress Cataloging-in-Publication Data
Stoddard, Alexandra.
[Tea celebrations]
Alexandra Stoddard's tea celebrations: the way to serenity / by Alexandra Stoddard
p. cm.
ISBN 0-688-13427-0
1. Afternoon teas I. Title. II. Title: Tea celebrations.
TX736.S76 1994 94-17054
641.5'3—dc20 CIP

Printed in the United States of America

First Edition

1 2 3 4 5 6 7 8 9 10

BOOK DESIGN BY MARYSARAH QUINN

ILLUSTRATIONS BY STEPHEN FREEBURG

To the memory of

Ruth Elizabeth Johns,

my aunt, who took me
around the world when I was sixteen
and opened my eyes to life, beauty, and tea

Contents

Great as has been the influence of the tea-masters in the field of art, it is as nothing compared to that which they have erected on the conduct of life. Not only in the usages of polite society, but also in the arrangement of all our domestic details, do we feel the presence of the tea-masters. Many of our delicate dishes, as well as our way of serving food, are their inventions.

They have taught us to dress only in garments of sober colors. They have instructed us in the proper spirit in which to approach flowers. They have given emphasis to our natural love of simplicity, and shown us the beauty of simplicity. In fact, through their teachings tea has entered the life of the people.

—OKAKURA KAKUZO
The Book of Tea

Chapter I

LOVE
AND THE
TEA
CEREMONY

The tea ceremony is more than an
idealization of the form of drinking —
it is a religion of the art of life.

— OKAKURA KAKUZO

Tea. Say the word and begin to breathe deeply. Sigh, knowing you'll experience a moment of tranquillity and elegance. With ever-greater chaos and noise all around us, we desperately need moments of peace, contentment, and grace. Tea and the tea ritual can satisfy this yearning. Tea is healing. It can be an aesthetic experience as well as a spiritual one. Tea is also mysterious, a metaphor for secret desires. It bestirs memories and lets us regain a sense of serenity. Tea is within reach for all of us.

As a little girl, I "played tea" with my friends. I had my own set of diminutive cups, saucers, and a teapot. They were the props for many scenes and acts in a play I couldn't grasp fully but in which the

> *It is a funny thing about life—if you refuse to accept anything but the best, you very often get it.*
> SOMERSET MAUGHAM

ways of grown-ups were imitated. Sometimes I was even allowed to serve real tea to my friends, but mostly I made do with water and a capacious imagination.

As I saw it then, tea was a social event that called for gracious posture, lively conversation, and Sunday clothes. It was an occasion that miraculously allowed this shy, awkward little girl to feel like a queen. Tea *is* grown-up, yet it is an occasion that sometimes includes children. As a young girl, I was not allowed to drink coffee. Tea, however, was acceptable and was offered to me as a treat.

Each of us, whether broken or whole, is empowered by tea. There is more to this drink than just the leaves from a *Camellia sinensis* bush. Tea brings us in closer touch with ourselves. It provides peaceful moments to reflect on our life's chapters as they unfold, and it allows us to be intimate with friends, co-workers, and loved ones.

As much as I loved to "play tea" with my little friends, I much preferred being included in adult tea parties. I have very early memories of joining my

4

mother both when she had tea alone with one special friend and when she got together with a group of friends. Ever since I was able to hold a cup in my small hands, I've participated in tea celebrations, adding up to almost a thousand over the span of half a century, and I can't remember one that was unpleasant. This can't be accidental. Looking back over the many chapters in my life, I realize I owe very much to tea.

Regardless of the flavor of the selected leaves, I see sipping tea, whether alone or in company, as a bridge that unites me to a wide variety of people. When we sit down with a cup of tea in our hands, we commune spiritually with fellow drinkers all over the world.

Most social activity centers on food and drink. I am certain that I can attribute my being comfortable in the company of very diverse people to being included in my parents' gatherings in my childhood. Since those early days, the tea celebration has been a mainstay in my life. Whenever an older person wished to counsel me, there would be tea. I didn't have a clue then what tea was or where it came from. All I knew was that I felt good whenever I heard the word or was invited to have some.

With tea amuses the evening, with tea solaces the midnight, with tea welcomes the morning.
SAMUEL JOHNSON

Several important events in my growing up have centered on tea. When I was seventeen, my parents gave a tea to *present* me to their friends and their friends' children. This custom was not uncommon then. Photographs commemorate the event. Quite properly, I was dressed in silk taffeta, with a velvet sash.

The period in my life that was most closely associated with tea was the winter of my sixteenth year, when I went around the world with Aunt Betty, my father's older sister, Ruth Elizabeth Johns. She had sent me boxes full of books to read in preparation for this life-transforming trip. I spoke of them in the Foreword to my book *Grace Notes: Insights, Reflections, Inspirations and Quests for Every Day of the Year.* Ever since, I have continued to study and be fascinated by Eastern philosophy and culture. Thinking back on those three months, everywhere we went, every party we attended, we were offered and served tea. Not only did my aunt not drink alcohol, she didn't approve of it for anyone and certainly would not have thought favorably of having young nieces drinking "spirits." Tea was the preferred beverage, and we were tea'd and entertained in thirty-three cities from India to Japan.

My aunt was an international social worker with a large network of acquaintances and friends everywhere we went. From the most humble hut at the end of a dirt path in Delhi, India, to a regal embassy, we were served tea. Because she was concerned about disease, my aunt cautioned me to drink only liquids that had been boiled. Tea, she added, was also medicinal.

Even then I understood the imbibing of tea to have a sacred element. More than a drink, tea is an invitation to enter into a transcendental experience that heightens awareness. One can enjoy peace and

Practice not-doing and everything will fall into place.
LAO-TZU

beauty while concentrating fully on the moment. You begin to catch a glimpse into the mystery of how each one of us influences and teaches others through the choices we make. I emerge from a tea ceremony a more centered person. Whether I'm by myself, or with a friend, or even at a tea party, I always find the experience enlightening and empowering.

Tea cuts across time; it is a bridge to old souls, sages, poets, philosophers, mystics, and Zen masters, people who I imagine have dedicated their lives to the quest for truth. Whenever anyone succeeds in awakening our sensibilities, we should pay our respects.

As a continuum in my life, tea weaves together memories of happiness as well as sorrow. When I was a small child, my mother used to spoon me warm tea laced with honey if I had a sore throat, a fever, or a cold. Whenever someone I love dies, tea is

the only beverage that soothes me, that connects me with others.

In 1959, my seventeenth year, when I was in the magical temple city of Kyoto, Japan, I participated in a ceremony in a tearoom presided over by a tea-master. That event planted the seeds of direction to my life. That afternoon I began to feel the vastness of what it means to be human, and I felt, even though I was young and ignorant, part of something larger than I was able to understand then. I became free of apprehension. I was at peace. What I took part in thirty-five years ago has fueled my faith and hope ever since.

In that quiet ten-foot-square wood-and-bamboo teahouse, with the sound of rapidly boiling singing water in an iron kettle in the background, I captured the essence of harmony. It dawned on me that everyday living can be transmuted from the mundane to the majestic, from the ordinary to the extraordinary, and that it is up to us to master this art. The way to do that, I believe, is to live each moment, each experience, with reverence. Everything matters because every-thing is connected. There is no beginning and no end, only the *now* is real—nothing can ever be more important. We can't learn this truth too soon.

Peter is convinced that in a former life I must have been an apprentice tea-master, because I feel such affinity for this ceremony. To my knowledge, since the sixteenth century when the tearoom was created by Rikiu, the greatest of all tea-masters, no computer, headset, earphone, telephone, or fax has been allowed through the garden path, the *roji*.

From very early on, I was taught to appreciate beauty, first by my mother, Barbara Green Johns, and my godmother, Martha Wood Christian, and later by my art teacher in high school, Phyllis Gardner. But this trip around the world did for me so much more than the occasional visit to the Boston Fine Arts Museum or to Isabella Gardner's palatial home in Fenway Court; this journey was an introduction to the mystery of polar opposites. The yin and the yang. I began to experience life in its complexity, noticing dramatic differences in peoples, in their interpretation of such notions as freedom, education, health, and power. I became aware of the influences of the East on the West, and vice versa.

As I reflect on Western and, increasingly, global values, I feel more and more certain that technology is *not* going to save us. We may all end up "progressing" to a premature death. We strive so hard to avoid

> Tea tempers the spirit and harmonizes the mind; dispels lassitude and relieves fatigue; awakens thought and prevents drowsiness.
>
> LU YU

listening to the demands of the soul. Once we get out of step with nature and fail to appreciate the gift of life, we diminish ourselves and those around us. That tea ceremony opened me up to exploration. I needed to learn to stop trying to nail down black-and-white answers. I understood that I understood *nothing,* and the certainty of this remains with me to this day. This knowledge does not  fill me with anxiety; rather, it fills me with peace. That afternoon so many years ago, I thought of my father. I felt sad thinking of his long daily commute to Manhattan, leaving his wife and children in the dark in a sleepy bedroom suburb and returning in the dark of night. There was little harmony or personal fulfillment in his routine.

I spent more time with the tea-master that afternoon than I had ever spent at one sitting with my father alone. What a stunning realization! The homecoming from the East was a shock to my system. I saw people hustling and bustling; no one seemed to make time to be still, to be reflective and look for the bigger picture.

I was forced to rely on my inner resources to try to find meaning in my life as I lived with people who hadn't had a taste of this enlightenment. I forgave  my father for being unable to be close, to communicate. He hadn't had the blessing of being exposed to the philosophy of the East, had never participated in a tea ceremony. He had no way of sharing my experience. I didn't even attempt to try to integrate myself back into my old ways of thinking and being. I couldn't. I was a different person. I found that very few people understood even the most basic concepts I was now compelled to live by. Those who did were also on a quest. I continued my studies privately. I learned to accept other people without trying to reform them.

Gradually, I became more sensitive and appreciative of the beauty that was around me, and I was able to gain perspective on my surroundings. I had no clear picture of what was to unfold for me, but I knew I was going to explore a life of the spirit and pay attention to the signs that would lead me to an appreciation of art as a way of life.

What is it about this tea ceremony that took place so long ago that haunts me to this day? Why, here in my garden, several thousand miles away and many years later, do I recollect, as if it were yesterday, the calmness I attained in the Zen temple? My father is dead, his sister, Aunt Betty, is dead.

We can only live in a state of grace when we are serene. The tea ceremony is symbolic for me; a proof that when we pay attention to little things a universal energy flows through our present, magnifying the meaning of events.

I often think about my mother and her influence on me. She had not had the opportunity to travel outside of the United States at an early age, as I did at sixteen. I'm certain she was skeptical regarding our experience. After all, this was not my mother's adventure, but a journey led by her husband's older spinster sister. On my return, I could never properly impress on her the impact of the tea ceremony on my psyche and what I had absorbed in my three months of travel in the East.

I suppose no person ever enjoyed with more relish the infusion of this fragrant leaf than did Johnson.

JAMES BOSWELL

13

But somehow, through osmosis, time, and my enthusiasm, my mother came close to understanding the essence of my experience. And it wasn't until she went to Japan herself, twenty years later, that everything fell into place for her. The fact that I had woven this experience into my life and my work brought us closer together.

The "art of tea" is a spiritual force for us to share.
ALEXANDRA STODDARD

I began to trust that most things that matter can be learned from tea-masters. Their goal is to inform daily life with meditation and high standards of refinement. Okakura Kakuzo, in his masterpiece book that was first published in America in 1906, wrote of tea-masters:

> In all circumstances serenity of mind should be maintained, and conversation should be so conducted as never to mar the harmony of the surrounding . . . for until one has made himself beautiful he has no right to approach beauty. Thus the tea-master strove to be something more than the artist—art itself. It was the Zen of aestheticism. Perfection is everywhere if we only choose to recognize it.

A tea-master is an interior designer, an architect, a gardener, a flower arranger, a textile artist, a ceramic artist, a philosopher, a musician, and, most important, a master of the art of living. That human beings can perfect their aesthetic sense, shape their attitudes, and become more in tune with the present moment is our privilege. Noticing the subtle beauty that surrounds us in the intimate moments of every day should spur us to find meaning in the smallest things. As Saint Catherine of Siena observed, "Heaven is along the way."

Life, as she aptly put it, is a process, not a result. We can never make up for past loss. When we fully concentrate on what we're doing, allowing circumstances to influence and inspire us to make changes that reflect our current mood, we will feel sublimely alive.

The purpose of Zen is the perfection of character.

YAMADA ROSHI

I'm beguiled by the idea that *life* can be *art.* We can create beauty in everything we do. We can tackle with feeling all aspects of our daily lives. This commitment to quiet grace, to hearing a symphony in the rustle of leaves and in the bubble of water boiling for tea, to finding elation in the sight of a single purple-blue morning glory climbing the garden wall, turns existence into art.

The tea ceremony is an example of what is possible, here, now, every day. It presents us with an opportunity to think about who and what is important, and invites us to seek beauty in friends, in simplicity, in nature, in humility, and in change. This experience as a teenager gave me enormous hope that my life could be lived beautifully, and that so much of the quiet refinements available to all of us each day must not be overlooked in the drive for a future goal.

The tea ceremony developed from the Zen ritual. "Zen" means meditation. Zen followers strive for communion with the inner essence of things. Zen masters believe that the banal and the spiritual are equally important. Everything, large and small, matters. At the core of Zen is the belief that greatness lies in the potential for everyday events to transcend the ordinary.

The founder of Taoism, Lao-tzu, lived five centuries before Christ. Taoism is recorded as the "art of being in the world." Okakura Kakuzo says "for

Tea—the cups that cheer but not inebriate.

WILLIAM COWPER

[Taoism] deals with the present—ourselves. It is in us that God meets with Nature, and yesterday parts from tomorrow. The present is the moving Infinity, the legitimate sphere of the Relative. Relativity seeks Adjustment; adjustment is Art. The art of life lies in a constant readjustment to our surroundings."

Lao-tzu teaches us the need to understand the whole so as to have greater control over the parts. His favorite metaphor is of the vacuum, illustrating that an empty water pitcher is beautiful because it is a vessel for water, and not because of the beauty of its shape or the materials used in the making of it. The beauty lies in the vessel's potential.

The tearoom, for example, provides space. This is more important than the fact that it consists of four walls joined by a roof. Okakura Kakuzo points out that "truth can be reached only through the comprehension of opposites." The steeped tea leaves are not as significant to the soul as the time and space and beauty associated with the ritual.

The tea ceremony provides an opportunity for meditation, concentration, and direct communication with the inner nature of things. And through this experience, each of us is given a chance to awaken to sacred secrets, to "be" rather than appear.

Dr. Stephen Addiss, professor of art history at the University of Kansas, wrote a beautiful introduction to *The Art of Zen.* "Zen teaches us not merely to hear, but to listen; not just to look, but to see; not only to think, but to experience; and above all not to cling to what we know, but to accept and rejoice in as much of the world as we may encounter."

Sudden enlightenment is, of course, rare. I haven't consciously experienced it once in these thirty-five years. But I do sometimes catch rays of light, here and there, when I awaken to my own nature and feel serene and harmonious.

If this fascinating plant we call tea can aid in restoring balance and tranquillity into our lives, it is certainly worth our attention. Tea brings clarity. Whatever the occasion, tea requires mindfulness. We must be present to experience the moment. When we sip tea, we are on our way to serenity. Tea. Aahh.

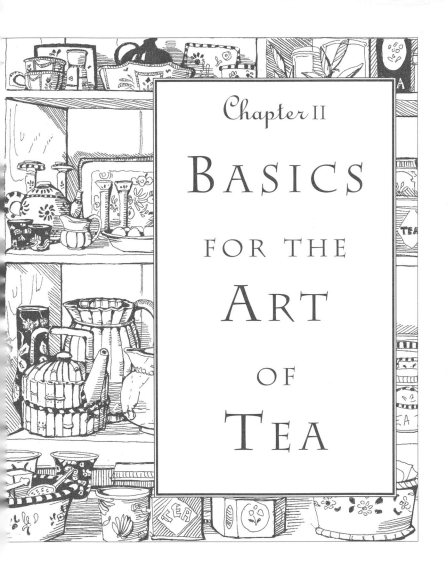

Chapter II

BASICS

FOR THE

ART

OF

TEA

*There is a great deal of poetry
and fine sentiment in a chest of tea.*

—RALPH WALDO EMERSON

Tea is always a ceremony. For this reason, it must be
approached in a certain way. Whether you're preparing a cup of tea simply because you're tired and
need a lift or planning a tea party in the garden,
there are certain things that are constants. The surroundings of the tea ceremony are almost as important as the tea itself. I will be discussing tea in a wide
variety of settings and occasions, but certain princi-
ples apply to each event.

Beauty matters. The tea-master teaches us that
everything is important. Because the tea celebration
is an opportunity for personal expression, let each
ritual reflect your spirit. Think of yourself as a tea-
master. Become a tea-master. With discipline and

care, you will refine each detail and come to value each step, each utensil, every cup and saucer, as symbols of something far greater than originally imagined.

The Book of Tea by Okakura Kakuzo discusses the Taoist and Zen concepts of perfection. "The dynamic nature of their philosophy laid more stress upon the process through which perfection was sought than upon perfection itself. True beauty could be discovered only by one who mentally completed the incomplete. The virility of life and art lay in its possibilities for growth. In the tea-room it is left for each guest to imagine the total effect in relation to himself."

Each tea-master creates his own aesthetic—selecting art, flowers, pottery, and poetry that appeals to him, much the same way we decorate the rooms in our houses. You can't please everyone, not even when serving tea. But I've discovered that when you can please yourself, you are giving of yourself.

See without looking; hear without listening; breathe without asking.

W. H. AUDEN

It has long been my belief that we can give authentically only what we experience honestly. If we like something and are excited and feel joy, chances are our enthusiasm will be infectious and our guests will respond positively.

Try to create original tea cele-brations. Customarily, tea-masters attempt to create an atmosphere that takes into consideration the season and the guests. Each tea ceremony is fresh and has a life of its own. Ideally, there should be no  repetition of theme, color, or shapes. This is so dif-ferent from the traditional English tea tray that dis-plays a matching set of teacups and saucers, com-plete with a matching teapot, water pitcher, cream and sugar containers.

Beauty must provide stimulation and originality. When I was a young girl, Aunt Betty would bring me teaspoons from her travels around the world. And often she'd give me a teacup and saucer, so, early on, I was exposed to the concept of one-of-a-kind. When I began collecting, I didn't have much money, so I followed her example and bought one wonderful cup and saucer at a time. What's impor-tant is to realize that there are infinite possibilities when you have variety in your inventory. Buying a set of anything seems somehow less exciting than finding, piece by piece, porcelain and pottery you respond to and love.

The same is true of teapots. Anyone who loves tea and its lore has a collection of teapots. The pots, provided one has ample space in one's cupboards, become friends and repositories of our memories. In the kitchen, we have an old pine corner cabinet hanging next to a tavern table and ladder-back chairs. Simply looking up at our collection fills us with pleasure. The teapots are wonderful together, even though each is different from the next. Their spouts and handles unify the group harmoniously.

Two of my favorite teapots were hand-painted for me by my friend Anne Gordon, a renowned potter. She gave them to me on two separate occasions. They are both in Wedgwood bone china. One has butterflies on either side of a painted plaque hanging down from the top, which reads simply: "Mrs. Brown's Tea Pot." Above is a series of bees, fruit, and honey. The handle is decorated with a series of tiny bees; the spout has snails and several little crawly creatures. On the back of the pot, there is a graceful swan spreading her wings, emulating Peter's family crest and my adaptation for the logo of my firm, Alexandra Stoddard Incorporated.

The other creation Anne Gordon made for me springs from nature. The pot is decorated with large leaves in various shapes and shades of green. Because everything she does is unique, the creamer goes with the pot but doesn't match it. Anne also enjoys making porcelain leaf dishes, which I use with this teapot for either lemons and limes or lemon cookies.

Aesthetically, these pots sing even when not filled. They are also practical. At the mouth of the spout, there is a built-in strainer so the leaves do not spill into the cup. But I'm not so practical that I would forfeit grace and elegance. Many of my teapots are faience or Quimper, and they as well as some others do not have this feature. Smaller individual pots rarely have the strainer. If you are attracted to a pot that doesn't have one, for a dollar or two you can

Teachers open the door; but you must enter by yourself.
CHINESE PROVERB

buy a strainer ball (in two sizes) at Williams-Sonoma or at almost any housewares store.

For lovers of *real* tea, a few leaves floating in the cup are not unpleasant. After all, how can our future be read if we use a sachet or tea bag?

A sterling-silver teapot would not look right in our old hanging pine cabinet. There is plenty here to create an aesthetically pleasing experience without having silver out tarnishing in the sea breeze. If I did have silver, it would probably be put away most of the time, which would be a shame. We gave our inherited silver tea sets to our church, where they are, blessedly, in constant use.

> You cannot be friends upon any other terms than upon the terms of equality.
> WOODROW WILSON

We have majolica teapots with whimsical decorations and appealing colors, also serious teapots from China and Japan. Even a few miniature pottery teapots in the shape of a watermelon, a strawberry, a cabbage, an artichoke. These wee trompe l'oeil vessels add amusement to the collection. They are just for show and add a bit of joy to the tray. Sometimes I hide a few jelly beans or M&M's inside, to amuse those who are tempted to lift off the tiny lids. . . .

What's wonderful about the tea celebration is that each of us may bring to it our own tradition and personal preferences. We needn't serve tea the same way our grandparents did. It would be sad if we felt we had to re-create slavishly parties of yore. What makes the ceremony sacred is what we bring to it of ourselves.

Each occasion is special. Every time you plan a tea happening, certain dynamics come into play. Listen and hear the message. For long after the event, there is a lingering intimacy. Three sips into a sincere tea ritual could change our attitudes about the way we choose to live our lives.

Paying attention is key. Having a variety of cups and saucers, teapots, creamers, and sugar bowls is a preamble. The best is yet to come. Before considering the tea itself, the accompanying food and sweets, the flowers and company, there are some essentials we must keep in mind and have on hand.

I love beauty that is also functional. Pitchers fit right into this category, and I've collected them over the years in a variety of shapes, sizes, glazes, and decorations. Some are crystal, some glass, clear and bubbly. Some are made of porcelain, stoneware, or

pottery. Unlike teapots, their spouts are short, and they have no lid. I am drawn to pitchers, vessels that are designed to hold and then pour.

What small delights I'm drawn to, wherever I travel, I find a way of purchasing and wrapping in my laundry and bringing home. All of our pitchers come from our trips; none has been purchased in a department store. Each one has behind it a memory, a spirit of place. These useful containers evoke nostalgic associations and have a place in my heart.

They are equally adorable whether sitting on the shelf, side by side, like soldiers, or being used enthusiastically at teatime.

A pitcher can be used for hot water, milk, iced tea, and if it is short and squat and the opening at the top is wide enough, it may hold a collection of cocktail napkins, spoons, iced-tea sippers, swizzle sticks, and even flowers. I can't remember a tea where we didn't put at least one of our beloved pitchers into action. Like the teapots, pitchers look handsome when arranged thoughtfully in a group. But more important than their presence on a pantry shelf, pitchers are inviting. Often, as I put the kettle on, I'll fill a pitcher with water and take care of some potted plants while I wait for the whistle.

Very often I snip off a few buds and place them in a tiny pitcher. Even when setting up a tray for myself, I enjoy a little blossom in a small jug. The handles of the pitcher and teapot elbow one another.

The paraphernalia of tea are so much a part of the attraction. Teacups and teapots are for piping-hot tea. But for approximately one third of the year, we prefer iced tea. Whenever it is too warm for us to have a fire in our bedroom, Peter and I usually prefer iced tea, with the exception of breakfast. Glasses, in all shapes, colors, and sizes, make the experience more enjoyable. As long as I can remember, my mother served iced tea from clear glasses with sterling-silver tea sippers. These silver "straws" with miniature spoons on the ends had holes in the center so one could use them to stir sugar and sip the cool tea. Mother often put slices of lemon, lime,

Zen in its essence is the art of seeing into the nature of one's being.
D. T. SUZUKI

31

and orange in the glass, as well as a sprig of mint; thus the spoon was also useful for stirring and even crushing the fruit against the sides of the glass. I got so much pleasure out of these iced-tea sippers that I was disappointed whenever I couldn't use one.

When Peter and I first went to Venice together with the girls, almost twenty years ago, we took a day trip to the islands of Murano and Burano, where glass and lace-making are treasured arts. Glass-blowing is fascinating to watch; my first encounter with this craft took place near Nice, in Biot. A secret formula allows the craftsmen to retain bubbles in the glass. While the Italians imitate this, there is nothing quite like an authentic Biot glass. When you watch

the firing, you feel you've bonded more fully with the pitcher, glass, or bowl you take home.

Murano is also magical. There the artists create colored "barber shop" candy-cane stripes of spun glass. The result is a feast for the eye. You want to put this wonder to use in your home. These stirrers come in varying sizes, appropriate for pitchers and for glasses. It would be impossible to hide them in a drawer; I always keep my collection in see-through pitchers on the kitchen counter, waiting for action. Just as beautiful as a painting or a floral arrangement, these colorful swizzles make up a bountiful bouquet that sparkles and delights even the weary. Over the years, we have added to our collection of Murano swizzles—to the amusement of our family and friends.

Italian swizzles can be bought in this country. When Peter and I were in Minneapolis on a recent trip, we were able to pick up some clear-stemmed ones with bright yellow stars at the top at Pier I. I've also seen there some pretty ones with blue balls, and they were reasonably priced. Of course, I bought some. Sometimes I put the blue ball at the bottom of the glass, and other times I put it at the top for color and delight. These decorative accessories add a great deal of spirit to the celebration and enjoyment of tea.

In 1959, in India, we were often served tea in clear glasses. Years later, after acquiring all these lively swizzles, I put the two together and served my friends hot tea in a glass, accompanied by a swizzle. It was fun, but not as exciting as drinking from hand-blown spun glass.

Whenever I can, I continue to add to my collection of glasses; I pick up unique pieces made by artists I discover at craft fairs around the country. At first Peter claimed he didn't like to drink out of anything but a traditional clear glass, but now he's grown to appreciate other, more imaginative kinds of glasses.

In the last several years, there has been a great variety of glass to choose from. Artists are having a good time blowing color into fun forms and shapes. Some of these new designs are unusual, and they are pleasant to the eye and touch.

We have now acquired a number of these "funky" glasses, and we enjoy using them for hot tea. When we select a swizzle that complements the colors of the rim of the glass, or that matches the polka dots on the glass itself, we have the makings of some fun.

Life is serious. Tea is serious. But we can also play and have humor in the process. I'm certain that the combination of a colorful glass with a swizzle makes the tea zestier and the spirit lighter.

Everything that is amusing and artistic and aesthetic is appropriate for the tea ceremony. I love to cup my hands around the porcelain or glass, warm them, and, with elbows on the table, look, listen, and be entertained by a kindred spirit. I pay no attention to etiquette. My elbows are on any available surface, whether it be a desk, a dining table, or a table set up for tea. If I am lowering standards for the socially correct or proper, so be it. The pure pleasure I derive from being with my elbows planted on something firm is worth it. In a formal Japanese or English tea party, we have no choice, but these occasions are rare. We are therefore fortunate to express our natural inclinations on a regular basis.

Earth's crammed with heaven.

ELIZABETH BARRETT BROWNING

The tea experience is an opportunity to open ourselves to fresh ideas. What was appropriate for Granny may seem ridiculous now. If we are flexible and seek new ways of expression, we will find greater serenity than if we insist on imitating behavior that is not suitable in present circumstances.

Tea is drunk to forget the din of the world.

T'IEN YIHENG

Continually, we have to remember Shakespeare's words, "To thine own self be true." It would be awful if we felt we had to put on airs in order to serve tea to friends. Let's concentrate on defining ourselves, not on keeping obsolete customs alive. My grandparents were dead before my eighth year. I'd be scared to have them over for tea in our home today. They'd need to be warned that things have changed. Life doesn't stand still, and neither does the tea ceremony. If all Americans were to stop what they are doing every afternoon around four o'clock and were to have tea, there is no telling what societal repercussions this new custom would have! However, sipping commercial tea from a Styrofoam cup with a tea-bag string hanging over the edge would be very depressing, if that is what the tea break were to amount to.

Aside from the cups and saucers, pots, pitchers, glasses, and swizzles, an important element of the tea ceremony is the tray. If my grandmother could see me now, perhaps she'd be shocked. While I appreciate the English silver tea service and the Taoist wooden slab of a tray with earthy pottery mugs, I prefer brightly colored gallery trays. The colors express my sense of joy. Whenever I am served from a silver tray, I am impressed, because it is not something I could carry off easily. We have a silver tray or two, but the parts don't add up to a cohesive whole.

Trays can be wonderful. A simple wood tray, if beautiful, provides a good backdrop for cups and saucers. Whether you're carrying tea into the garden in the summer or resting a tray in front of a cozy fire, select it with care. Having several different-size trays made of a variety of materials helps you to continually vary your presentation. We have several old wood trays ranging from a large, sturdy mahogany butler's tray to a substantial elm-burl one with a pretty brass gallery. We enjoy cheerfully painted  contemporary wood trays reminiscent of Henri Matisse, too, as well as gallery trays of wicker and Oriental lacquer.

To add a touch of refinement, I often put a cotton or linen place mat on the bottom of the tray, but this depends on the look I wish to achieve. When we use our beautiful early nineteenth-century English tray of gleaming wood and brass, I resist covering it up. I pick up old, fine cotton place mats at country antique fairs for a few dollars. They look pretty on a contemporary tray. Sometimes I use a large dinner napkin, so that some of the cloth cascades over the sides of the tray.

Peter likes trays that have some kind of handle; he feels more comfortable using those. It is practical to have trays with galleries of approximately one and a half to two inches, because if you bang your tray into a doorframe, you may spill, but you won't have to mop the floor.

Go on loving what is good, simple and ordinary.
RAINER MARIA RILKE

Take stock of your tray collection. There is no need for a tray to be boring either in color or design. Acrylic paints come in dozens of colors, and you can sand and spray-paint a tray in less than ten minutes. If yours are nicked or dreary, consider the pleasure of upgrading your trays. We hang the decorative painted trays in our kitchen faceup and think of them as part of the decor.

An important part of the tea ritual is a cotton cocktail napkin. It's a grace note worthy of the time it takes to wash and iron them, and the ironing is part of the whole process. Lovely cloth napkins are pleasing to the touch and should be used. If you buy even an average package of paper cocktail napkins, you will discover they cost at least ten cents each. Not only does this add up, but it is never as special as the real thing, and moreover it is not ecological.

Most of us have inherited some old linen from a grandmother, an aunt, or our mother. These small napkins when spray-starched are not only nostalgic but a symbol of serenity, reminding us of a less stressful, slower-paced existence. Because my parents are dead, I have inherited a large selection of their linen. We have a closet in our dining room that has shelves

> But friendship is precious, not only in the shade, but in the sunshine of life; and . . . the greater part of life is sunshine.
>
> THOMAS JEFFERSON

where I lay out my treasured inheritance. Every time I go into that closet, I play; I take out a stack, make my selection, and caress each piece lovingly. These small pieces of textile have a *real* immortality. They are alive because we use them regularly. Your guests may be too shy or polite to use your finest hand towels, but they will definitely use these dainty and ele-gant reminders of times past.

Look in your linen closet and see if anything is yellowing and could benefit from some Clorox 2. Soak and wash them with a favorite bar of fragrant soap. I especially love lemon-, almond-, and jasmine-scented soap when I wash delicate linens. Because I iron only when the spirit moves me, usually when it rains, I listen to the sound track from the movie *Mission*. I turn on bright lights and spend a few minutes pressing my treasures. This process never seems to fail. When I unplug the iron and bring my pretty stack down the back staircase and into the closet, I feel light as air and wonder why it's still raining. I select my favorite napkin and go put the kettle on for some tea.

Recently, Brooke, Peter, and I went to an annual antiques fair at a local school, where we found a wonderful selection of these small gems. Buy one for twenty-five cents at a town fair. Don't worry about size, color, or quantity. Jump in and enhance your collection. There are perfectly beautiful contemporary cocktail napkins that you can find in fine linen departments in stores, but they are often painfully expensive. I've indulged in these from time to time. Usually, they are sold in sets tied with ribbons. Some napkins have a half-inch contrasting colored trim all around. For those of us who enjoy sewing, get your inspiration and go with it. Sewing a washable grosgrain ribbon all around a cotton square is easy handwork. You simply bind the edge so half shows on each side, front and back, and you miter the edge.

For my taste, the most beautiful contemporary cocktail napkins are made in France by Porthault Linens. These small-scale designs have a hand-scalloped, hand-rolled, hand-sewn border in a contrasting welt on all four sides. These are not for everyone, and at approximately twenty dollars apiece they might be out of the reach of most of us, but I am passionate about them. Examining the tiny little perfect stitches brings me

Thought is action in rehearsal.

SIGMUND FREUD

41

great pleasure. I confess I have gathered a handful of these over more than thirty years and don't have two that are alike. It would seem redundant to have any match, because I enjoy having a garden of colors and patterns to look at. The fine cotton is soft and gentle. When the girls were little, I had a baby pillow for their carriage with the same scalloping all around. I love getting the nose of the iron into each scallop. By using heavy spray starch, I can get the border to stand up so it shows on all four sides. Just bringing one of these tiny napkins to the tea ceremony awakens memories a quarter-century old.

Anything more than the truth would be too much.

ROBERT FROST

I can recall a tablecloth my mother used for a tea party when I was eight. It was made in Madeira, Portugal, and was white with hand-embroidered flowers in blues, pinks, and yellows with green leaves. I was struck by the sheer beauty of this material as it caught the afternoon sunlight in the garden.

Mother loved to have tea out in her garden in the summer, and on that day she had some lovely sweet peas in a white pitcher on the table. I remember sitting with Mother and my godmother, listening to them talk about antiques rather than playing because I was enthralled by the beauty of the tea table.

The table was in round wicker, convenient because it was lightweight and easy to bring out onto the lawn. A great pleasure at teatime is dressing the table. I've inherited a genuine love of fabric from my mother. While our taste differed greatly when it came to decorating, her tablecloths for the tea ceremony were my favorites, perhaps because they were all white or had white backgrounds.

Making table covers is easy and inexpensive if you can find a remnant of a fabric you adore. I've always made my own cloths. The only exception is if I buy beautiful white embroidered ones inexpensively in antique shops or at fairs. I love to throw a beautiful cloth over a table to create a mood of elegance and luxury. Furniture manufacturers might disagree, but the wood needs clothing, just as our bodies do.

Perhaps one of the reasons we have lost our inner peace is because we are so willing to sacrifice luxuries. Aren't we depriving ourselves of the things that turn our lives into art? When I wrote *Living a Beautiful Life,* I suggested that one of the ways we can enhance our lives is by paying attention to the things we do repeatedly, such as eating, sleeping, and bathing. If we find delight in adding a touch of elegance, order, joy, and beauty to every day, we will live more fully. But what often happens is that we shortchange ourselves of grace notes by not turning repetitive actions into refreshing experiences.

We can't afford to abandon our tablecloths to a dark closet and bring them out only a few times a year. When I look at a stack of folded tablecloths on the shelf, my heart becomes flooded with memories.

They're too pretty to hide. I need the elegance, refinement, and luxuriousness these simple pleasures provide. These yards of attractive printed cottons come alive only when I use them. Let's take them out of their storage place and let them breathe. If we never open ourselves up to the *big* picture, we will limit ourselves to believing that the humdrum is all there is. Tea provides us with one gate to the infinite.

Our own contribution is vital if an experience is to have depth, be meaningful. If we are too busy, or unwilling to perform certain tasks that are an integral part of the tea ceremony, we will never achieve master quality. It is our commitment that transforms the act into a ceremony, life into art.

Isn't serenity, after all, the result of creating meaningful rituals, the ability to go through a maze of experiences, face the labyrinth, and emerge tranquil? Serenity has a ripple effect. The napkins or tablecloth I use today and then launder and iron, fold and put away, are the cornerstones of future celebrations. These seemingly trivial things are what we must focus on now in order to point ourselves toward the light.

The truths that we must honor are simple if we are going to find serenity. There are no shortcuts. If we allow our lives to rush out of control, we will fuel our anxiety and distance ourselves from contentment.

The tea ceremony is here for us to participate in. It is a way to get in touch with our deeper selves and our potential.

For a tea-master, every aspect of the tea ritual is sacred. It was Lao-tzu who said over twenty-five hundred years ago, "The journey of a thousand miles begins with one step." All we have to do is take the first tiny step. Dr. Samuel Johnson believed that "the *process* is the reality." Is it such a big thing to plug in an iron and spend a few minutes straightening out the wrinkles in a favorite cloth? This mundane activity should be cherished because it is done in anticipation of something special.

Ecstasy is a glass full of tea and a piece of sugar in the mouth.

ALEXANDER PUSHKIN

While we are alive and able, we can create ceremonies that lead us toward serenity. To become enlightened is to be supplied with light. The dictionary definition is "to illuminate, to make shine, to enkindle. To shed the light of truth and knowledge upon us; to furnish with increase of knowledge; to instruct; also to supply with spiritual light." There are basics to the art of tea. Often these truths are sitting among us.

Flowers are angels rooted in soil. People often think of heaven as up in the distant sky, but some of us believe it is "along the way." Here, we can cultivate our own garden. Flowers are so important, I am frightened to think of life without them. Flowers are a focal point to every tea ceremony of mine.

Whether you are alone with one blossom or an African violet plant at your side in the dead of winter, or at a tea party in a garden in full bloom on a summer afternoon, flowers are here to remind us of our inner garden. They are purveyors of color, beauty, and life.

We can't postpone our appreciation of flowers for some future time. A daylily lives only one day. Some flowers are annuals and some are perennials, but they will not blossom year after year. Flowers urge us to look at them, and by the brevity of their lives they force us to examine what it means to be on this human journey.

Pay attention to your flower and plant containers. Ivy put in a hand-painted earthenware cachepot can be far more attractive than an expensive floral

arrangement that looks contrived. One short-cropped rose, open-faced in a bud vase, can have more impact than a fancy bouquet that doesn't express a personal aesthetic. The bigger your selection of vases, the greater your enjoyment will be. In our buttery off our kitchen, we have shelves filled with vases as well as cachepots and pitchers.

Playing with flowers has been a lifelong passion for me. The time spent creating something artistic and fresh is healing and should not be rushed. When we treat flowers with tenderness, this calm and grace affects our soul. The tea ritual, above all else, teaches us to care about what we're doing. The empty containers, like the empty tearoom, are the vacuums that make the experience possible.

The Japanese sensibility is highly refined. The word *shibui* means subtle beauty filled with mystery, reverence, and grace. As we explore the ways of the tea-master, we can look upon the art of flower arranging through his eyes. Don't create anything symmetrical. Be sparing in your selection. Never use more flowers than absolutely necessary for the desired effect. Show some of the stem and leaves as well as the bloom. Play. The vessel should be half as tall as the flowers from the bottom of the stem to the top of the arrangement. Vary the stem heights as much as you can. Always have a leaf or blossom overlapping the vase.

Don't forget about water glasses, both clear and colored, for your bouquets. Earthenware mustard pots are also good. Gather one-of-a-kind finds in thrift shops, flea markets, and country fairs. Each treasure will add to your inspiration. When you use a jar with a lid, place the lid next to the arrangement as part of the composition. Use a flat dish to hold a series of tiny buds. And when it seems appropriate, make a colorful grouping in a tulip teacup or favorite coffee mug.

When the spirit moves me, I arrange flowers in an old brass watering can. Put them in a teapot, a brandy snifter, or a saki cup, and remember the art of ikebana (flower arranging) can be a lifelong inspiring experience that enhances the senses and relaxes the mind and makes the spirit soar. Just the other day I arranged some yellow

Work is love made visible.
KAHLIL GIBRAN

49

roses in a bright blue tea caddy. Sometimes Peter helps me; he likes to play with flowers, too.

With the understanding of all the elements that make up the tea ceremony, all that is left to consider is the kettle, the water, and the tea. I have a bright blue whistling teakettle, purchased at Williams-Sonoma. Just as altitude and climate affect the quality of the evergreen *Camellia sinensis* bush, the quality of the water used affects the quality of the tea. I boil cold tap water. It shouldn't come as a surprise to you to know that the better the water, the better the tea. We are fortunate in the East to have good water flowing from our kitchen faucets.

> *It is a mistake to look too far ahead. Only one link in the chain of destiny can be handled at a time.*
> SIR WINSTON CHURCHILL

To become a serious tea-master, you should consider hand-picked full-leaf teas. The top two leaves and bud produce the most flavorful tea. Some go so far as to use just the bud. I am, however, not a purist. I've been known to grab a tea bag. Who among us hasn't? I always travel with a bunch. This way I'm able to have whichever tea I'm in the mood for. I don't like to be dependent on the bland, boring

breakfast tea bags normally provided by hotels or restaurants.

> *True contentment is the power of getting out of any situation all that there is in it.*
> G. K. CHESTERTON

Loose tea is not only finer, but it
is also more economical. Making a
sachet or tea bag is labor-intensive.
Some people feel it is not as healthy
as sipping loose tea leaves. Tea bags
are a convenience, but the ceremony is more sensuous when we make tea from a tin. Most companies
sell tea in reusable tins—of course, the refills are less
expensive.

There are three categories of tea: black tea, black
blended tea, and green tea. Herbal teas are caffeine-
free and don't come from the evergreen plant
Camellia sinensis. I embrace all possibilities and also
enjoy herbal infusions enormously.

Start where you are. Open your cabinet and take
your tea inventory. I did this and put thirty-three tea-
bag cartons in a wicker basket. I was amazed how
much tea in bags I have. As you can see, I buy the
tea from many different suppliers, and I enjoy them
all in different ways. Each company has a slightly
different way of processing its tea or packaging it.
The variety is marvelous, and it is a feast to the eye. I

have particularly enjoyed the round little tea bags of the Republic of Tea. So here are the contents of my basket:

Ahmad Tea, London	Thé de Ceylon
Bigelow	Perfect Peach (herbal tea)
	Earl Grey
	English Teatime (decaffeinated)
Celestial Seasonings	Cinnamon Rose
	Mandarin Orange Spice
	Red Zinger
	Lemon Zinger
	Spearmint
	Almond Sunset
	Cinnamon Apple Spice
	Chamomile
	Raspberry Patch
	Bengal Spice
Grace Tea Company	Fancy Ceylon
	China Yunnan
	Russian Caravan

Health and Heather	Night Time
	Mixed Fruit
	Lemon Grove
	Wild Black Currant
	Grapefruit and Orange
J. H. Ford Tea Company, Inc.	Jasmine
	Keemun
	Jubilee
	Fruit Ambrosia
	Lemon Cooler
	Cinnamint
Pompadour	Rosehip and Hibiscus Flowers
	Earl Grey
	Ceylon Orange Pekoe
	English Breakfast Tea
The Republic of Tea	Lapsang Souchong
	Malty Assam
	Jasmine Jazz
	Big Green Hojicha
	Moroccan Mint
	Ginseng Licorice
Tea Masters of London	Tea for Me
	English Breakfast
Twinings	China Oolong

Twinings (cont.)   Darjeeling
                                    Orange Pekoe
                                    Irish Breakfast
                                    English Breakfast

But I've discovered I'm now equally interested in loose tea, thanks in part to the Republic of Tea. A few "teaists," a word coined by Okakura Kakuzo, started a company whose mission is to teach people how to "live and work, sip by sip rather than gulp by gulp." These successful businesspeople see themselves as "tea spirits." Not only do they sell their full-leaf teas in attractive tins that hold enough tea for sixty or more cups, they make the lore of tea fun by giving each tea an association, printed on the reusable tin. For example, Lapsang Souchong is "The Tea of Mystery," Malty Assam "Back in the Body Tea," Cinnamon Plum "Tea of Conviviality," and Ginger Peach "Longevity Tea." The Republic of Tea's descriptions of each tea are both fun and educational.

I particularly like green teas, because they are less strong than black teas, and I find them soothing.

The Dragon Well green tea, for example, is "Lao-tzu's tea," a famous green cooling tea. Not bad company to keep when we open ourselves up to the associations. The water is bubbling. It's time to select a tea, set up a tray, and have a tea celebration for one.

Chapter III

TEA

FOR

ONE

I am in no way interested in immortality,
but only in the taste of tea.

—Lu T'ung

When you have flowers, books, and tea, you are never alone. In these quiet moments when I take a break, I feel like a compass, returning to magnetic north.

Katharine Hepburn, I've read, takes up to five baths a day. Pierre Bonnard's wife, Maria, loved baths, and because of his affection for her, he would often sit with her while she soaked in the tub and paint her. Like taking a bath, creating a tea celebration for *one* is a soothing, comforting ritual. Whether we are in our own home or an office or hotel room, we must always rely on our inner resources.

I look forward to my tea for one; I think of it as

part of what I call *my* ten percent time. I need it. I
plan for it and I embrace it, every day. The mere fact

that I schedule at least one ceremony for one each day makes me a
more content, tranquil person. I
know, with certainty, that I will have
time alone to meditate, sip tea,
reflect, and even daydream. I

couldn't live without these private times. I can't
imagine that other people don't need them, too.

Tea, a drink over five thousand years old, is more
than a beverage. Tea is a way to live more deliberately.
When we sip tea, we open ourselves up to the natural
harmony of our bodies and the universe. Having a
tea ceremony alone each day, once or twice, gives
each of us an opportunity to refresh ourselves, to
appreciate what we have with new awareness and
mindfulness, and to center our minds, bodies, and
spirits.

Rituals are essential to humans, and yet somehow we've distanced ourselves from ceremony, particularly when we are alone. Why is it that it is so
hard for so many people to *be,* rather than to do? If
our houses always have to be in order, errands done,

newspapers and magazines read, leaves raked, telephone calls returned, bills paid, letters answered, before we allow ourselves a personal moment to reflect, we will die without ever knowing one of the great secrets: time-out. Tea for one is time-out. Value this time; it is a preamble to everything else. When I decorate a room, I try to arrange the space around a focal point: a beautiful mantel, a piece of furniture of rare beauty, a painting, or a piece of sculpture. Tea is the focal point of my inner journey.

It is when I am alone that I learn about myself. Whenever you create something special for yourself, you are honoring yourself. Tea for one gives us a daily opportunity to evaluate, reevaluate, to come to grips with our feelings. With this ritual, it is possible, on a regular basis, to bring harmony and balance back into our lives.

> Out of clutter, find simplicity. From discord, find harmony. In the middle of difficulty lies opportunity.
>
> ALBERT EINSTEIN,
> "THREE RULES OF WORK"

Unfortunately, few Americans value this experience. Far too many people, conscientious, ambitious, and hardworking, won't, for whatever reason, give themselves permission to have a moment's peace. We need to learn to value ourselves as much as we appear to value others' opinions of us.

What we do alone, away from scrutiny, is the real us; it is what lies at the root of our ability to love and to live serenely. What I do when I am not observed is far more revealing than what I do when exposed to the view of other people. If I don't make time to take care of myself, how can I be of use to others? We can't give more than what we have.

> *Right now a moment of time is fleeting by! Capture its reality... become that moment.*
>
> PAUL CÉZANNE

In today's rush, privacy is not only a privilege but a necessity. When I was little, I'd go into the garden whenever I wanted to be alone. I didn't have a friend or family member remotely interested in weeding, planting, and watering, so I was assured time on my own. But as adults with a family and career, community work and friends, we have precious little time to ourselves. We will never find it; we must claim it; I have tea for one twice a day, sometimes more often. I don't have a set time or place, but usually I schedule one early-morning private moment, and often another one between afternoon and bedtime.

No one invites me to this ritual but me. And like everything else we care deeply about, we do it because it is a priority, a happy way to restore our spirits.

Tea for one requires of us a vital ingredient besides some hot water and tea leaves: caring. We have to treat ourselves with the same tender love and affection as we treat a spouse, a parent, a sibling, a friend, or a lover. Just as our thoughts have a profound effect on our actions and inactions, when we do something for ourselves alone, we send a signal to our soul that our life has value.

Last summer Peter and I were invited for lunch to a friend's house in New Jersey. When we arrived, we found the front door open, the music on, flowers in little bouquets, and iced tea in a pitcher on the terrace. Down in the hammock by the river was our friend Jean, who had made a small pot of tea for herself and had put it on a tray with a cup and saucer. She was allowing herself a Zen moment before her guests arrived. We chose not to disturb her, and we sat on her terrace and helped ourselves to a delicious iced tea with raspberries and fresh mint. Jean's choice of hot tea was Lemon Wintermint, rhapsodically labeled "Quiet the mind herb tea made of lemon grass, lemon verbena, lemon peel combined with rose petals and fresh mint to create a soft, luscious cup." She serves this tea instead of decaffeinated coffee because herbal teas are caffeine-free and lovely. It was a memorable experience, sitting overlooking her garden, nibbling on a Proustian madeleine and watching her enjoying some solitude.

While I have no set time frame, my tea ceremonies may last as long as one hour. If I am in my garden, I always go to a favorite spot, and when I'm inside, I sit near a window. I have a small square lacquered tray, black outside and red inside, which I often seem to gravitate to for setting up my ritual. I use a cotton or linen napkin as a tray cover. I pay close attention to my selections—what tea I pick, what cup or glass. Often when I have tea alone, I use a glass because I love using the swizzles. After I select

> Make it a rule of life never to regret and never to look back. Regret is an appalling waste of energy; you can't build on it.
>
> KATHERINE MANSFIELD

a glass or cup and saucer, I pick a small vase or pitcher. Just having one rose or tulip or daisy short-cropped on the tray is a reminder that now, right here, is an important time. And after my tea interlude, I emerge uplifted and invigorated.

This solitary time allows me to hear my inner voice and tap into my yearnings and clear away whatever doesn't ring true and feel right. We are in an ever-evolving flow of awareness. What we think and feel  and experience now will have an effect on the future. We pay a price for our beliefs and convictions. Everything has consequences.

Why are we, as a nation, so afraid to be alone? We want support, but we haven't properly understood the medicinal, spiritual value of being *alone* and *quiet.*

I don't listen to music while I sip my tea because I like to hear the sounds around me, sounds that are usually drowned out by too much noise and activity. The *tick-tock* of a brass carriage clock is a reminder that we and we alone can experience these precious moments when we lose track of time and place and become one with a universal consciousness. Joel, David, and Karl Schapira, co-authors of *The Book of Coffee and Tea: A Guide to the Appreciation of Fine Coffees, Teas and Herbal Beverages,* wisely advise us: *Don't hurry.* When making tea, you have only time.

If I put some honey in my tea, I might be visited by a passing bee that has come to join me through an open window. I like the *buzz-buzz* of an enthusiastic bee, and I will let this excited visitor have a taste from my spoon before I shoo my friend back out of doors. I try to bring to this ritual my full attention. I am aware existentially of what I'm experiencing, what images surge in my mind, and what is happening deep inside me.

In hospitals around the country, holistic medicine is beginning to be taken seriously. Stress-reduction and management classes are springing up everywhere. People are literally asked to savor a *raisin* for the first time. Many of us have eaten raisins in our cereal for years and yet have never known what a raisin really tastes like. Taste a cup of tea as you would a raisin, concentrate fully on its flavor, and feel its soothing properties.

I don't advocate that doctors offer tea as a prescription. I don't drink tea for my health. I know tea is good for me, but so is the commitment to myself, to my life, to my aesthetic sense. I can't separate the tea leaves from the water or the water from the adorable hand-painted pot or the perky flower or all those souls I will never know who help direct my thinking. This experience is purely personal. I don't invite anyone to join me. I deliberately face a window so I can be in my own world. I listen to silence.

Teach us delight in simple things.
RUDYARD KIPLING

If I've received a letter from a loved one, I'll put it unopened on my tea tray and save it for the moment I can linger over each sentence. I don't want to be seen or to see people. This is the time I can reconnect with my spirit, feel my breathing, and be empowered with an inner calm and serenity not possible otherwise.

The elegance of the tea ceremony alters the way

we see the world, and because we allow ourselves to become more sensitive and open, we can then improve the quality of the atmosphere around us, wherever we go or whatever we do.

I never close my eyes when I sip tea. I am not someone who likes the dark unless I am ready to go to sleep. Creating this quiet time coaxes me into relaxation. Many of us get so caught up in what we should be doing that even sitting in a chair requires effort. But after a week or two of establishing this sacrosanct time, we will find a sanctuary, an ideal spot based on our mood, the time of day, who else is in the house, the weather, and our fantasies. How we *feel* will guide us.

A word of caution regarding wishing for approval. This is not a ceremony we perform to impress others or to invite others to share in our thoughts or participate in the mystery. Until we can learn to do something beautiful only for ourselves, we will always be in a state of anxiety, frustration, and even anger, since we will not be fulfilling our unique needs. We all have to make time and space to

tap into the truths and beliefs that
shape our values and our character.
Once we acquire the habit of creating an oasis of beauty and tranquillity for ourselves, we will grow to
understand that this way to serenity
is our greatest gift to us, and by extension, to those
around us. They will be the beneficiaries of a greater
sense of ourselves and of our renewed energy. We
can't give unless we are at peace.

A cup of tea costs between eleven and fifteen
cents. Why do we invariably protest that it takes
money to live a beautiful life? We know better, and
we have to seize the opportunities that are available
to all of us: men, women, and children, old and
young, rich and poor, healthy and unhealthy. The
aroma alone of tea can transport us to exotic lands:
Ceylon, India, China, the Himalayas. We don't need
to go to the movies or rent a video. Instead, we can
sip tea in our own world.

In 1961, when I first began decorating profes-
sionally, many women clients told me that they felt
guilty sitting "unproductively" in their houses. I was
surprised. Since they weren't "working," they felt

they should at least have a busy social life. Why do we feel guilty if we are enjoying our own company? Who turned our houses into forever-neat traps where our "work" is never done? I don't suffer from neurotic guilt. I try to take pleasure in my time-out seven days a week.

I have no set agenda. Often I write in my journal. At other times, if I feel I've been with people too much and I'm talked and listened out, I select a favorite author and read something that requires my full attention. If Peter or the girls are watching television at night and I don't want the distraction, I might decide to have tea on my own. I might take an oil or herbal bath, and massage tiny drops of Origins' "Peace of Mind" into my temples and forehead. I'll then set up my tray in bed and have my ritual, propped up by lots of pillows.

The butterfly counts not months but moments and has time enough.
RABINDRANATH TAGORE

Bed is not only a place to sleep, it is a wonderful sanctuary to retreat to when you want to refresh yourself. Oprah Winfrey filmed me in our New York bedroom, sitting in bed and sipping tea from a wicker tray hand-painted with flowers. I have a different feeling about beds and bedrooms than many other people. I adore spending time in bed and feel it is like a throne. When I was asked by the producer of Oprah's show which is my favorite room in our apartment, I immediately said the bedroom. And while I like a lot of beautiful furniture, I can't imagine a more versatile, comfortable item in any home-furnishings line than the bed. So, without blushing, in front of thirty million viewers, I was filmed, sitting up in my bed with a cup of chamomile tea.

I love an evening alone in bed. For me it is a luxury to be able to spread out all my magazines and mail and bring in a tea tray and sit up in solitary splendor for several hours of relaxation, reading and catching up on correspondence. When I was a child, bed was off-limits other than for sleeping or nursing colds. Now it is a very special treat.

I highly recommend a bed tray. I have a wicker one with two deep wells on either side for magazines, newspapers, catalogs, and mail. This leaves enough space on the top for a teapot and a cup and saucer as well as room to write a letter or in a journal.

One of these evenings when I was having a tea celebration in bed, I realized how much more aware of smell I become when I am not distracted by music or conversation. By my bed I have *The Complete Book of Essential Oils and Aromatherapy* by Valerie Ann Worwood, which includes "over 600 natural, non-toxic and fragrant recipes to create health, beauty, and a safe home environment." In a brief statement before the Introduction, the author tells us:

> Essential oils are one of the great untapped resources of the world. The concentrated essences of various flowers, fruits, herbs, and plants have been used for centuries all over the world, but in modern times we have forgotten the power of these ancient medicines of the earth, preferring instead to use the products of perfume and chemical companies which imitate the natural fragrances and medicinal and cleansing properties of essential oils. Because the essential oils are so sweet-smelling, many people suppose their value is essentially one of charm and fragrance—but this is a mistake. Modern scientific research has proven that essential oils are potent, with remarkable medicinal

properties. . . . Unlike chemical drugs, essential oils do not remain in the body. They leave no toxins behind.

The tea ceremony for one allows me to get in touch with my interests. Many friends lament that they are interested in too many *different* things. It's hard, they say, to keep them all going. I don't think any of us can be too engaged in life.  Our intuition tells us what we are innately drawn to and what we find burdensome. Whenever I have tea alone, I am back with me, and, if I do this regularly, I achieve a greater understanding of what drives me.

Unfortunately, our society pushes us to go out and be seen. Nothing is wrong with socializing. But if we are with others more often than we are with ourselves, we will become increasingly nervous and edgy. We should pay attention to signals from our subconscious and make the appropriate changes in our life. If someone is out and about and "being seen," it doesn't necessarily indicate that someone is

thriving. Some of us accept social invitations out of habit and at times a false sense of duty. Remember, an invitation is also an opportunity to say no gracefully. Are we capable of planning tea for one and taking it as seriously as though we had asked a friend over?

We must not cancel on ourselves even when outside pressures mount, particularly not then. One of the reasons I don't have a set time each day for the tea ceremony is because I try to find the most propitious time. Sometimes I decide at an instant's notice that I need my teatime. One of the sad realities of large businesses today is, there is no place for people to rest quietly. I hear of employees hiding in the toilet with their feet up to escape being seen as they try to regain their composure. Where can *you* go? I think of tea *for me* as a private ritual at home, always possible. If we don't seize opportunities when they are within our reach, we will live lives that are far from serene.

Food is not an important feature of my tea ceremony for one, but it can be, depending on the circumstances. When I have tea, most of the time I don't include food. But there is the occasional time when I feel a strong impulse to have something sweet, sour, or salty, and then I put a small portion of what I want on my tray. I observe a rule to never interrupt the occasion to restock or add supplies. What I put on the tray is all I'll consume. Remember, no one else is eating the salted nuts or potato chips or cheese sticks or cookies but you. When I have tea alone, I might put one cookie on the tray on a small dish, or one piece of chocolate.

While there's tea, there's hope.

SIR ARTHUR PINERO

No matter what craziness is going on around us, we can carve out these vitally important, yet simple and economical private times of renewal and contemplation. The purpose of tea is to help us seek and maintain openness, inner calm, tranquillity, elegance, beauty, joy, grace, and serenity. It is a magical potion that, with a few deep breaths and sips, begins to transform our spirit. Here, we ease our fears rather than fuel them, because we connect with a greater reality. No matter how we feel entering this ceremony—irritable, edgy, grabby, greedy, or impatient—soon, we breathe and sip, smell and touch, think and feel with a renewed soul. We taste what we long for the most: feeling blessed to be alive and trusting that we will be strong and resourceful not merely to get by, but to feel the awesome power of being connected with the universal.

> By a tranquil mind I mean nothing else than a mind well ordered.
>
> MARCUS AURELIUS

When I sip cinnamon-flavored tea, I am magically transported to the farm of earlier days when I picked apples with the girls and then went back to the kitchen to bake apple pies. Cinnamon and apples are linked in my brain. The Body Shop now sells nutmeg-and-cinnamon-flavored lip gloss that I sometimes buy because of these fond associations. After a bath, I spray an orange, tangerine, lemon, or lime moisturizer and then have tea in these citrus flavors as well. I also like other fruit flavors, such as pears, apricots, bananas, and peaches. Dr. Alan R. Hirsch, director of the Smell and Taste Treatment and Research Foundation in Chicago, has had success treating migraine patients, insomniacs, and anxiety sufferers with inhalants of green apple, banana, or vanilla. Hirsch theorizes that something in these foods either changes the neurotransmitters in the brain or increases alpha waves to produce a more relaxed state.

Since we apply our favorite scents to our body and often use the same ones to perfume our rooms, isn't it natural then that we would also enjoy these aromas in our tea and in the nibbles that we have with it? Think of some of the beauty treatments you like that use fruits or vegetables. Avocado facials or macadamia-nut-oil mascara or sesame oil for hands. I am sorry that  some people are allergic to these wonderfully uplifting smells and have to select scent-free products.

I love to put spices and herbs in my cooking because they add zest to what I am preparing. A little nutmeg on spinach is a favorite. I glaze carrots in orange juice and shave the rind in with parsley, honey, and cinnamon. I often use raspberry vinegar with olive oil as my basic dressing, which I then enhance with lemon and lime juice, freshly ground pepper, and mustard. In tea we can endlessly experiment with flavors and smells. What a waste to be a purist, especially when you are doing these things for yourself.

Just as you try different bath oils, gels, soaps, and perfumes that are comforting, do the same with tea. Be daring! My friend Lin Shay owns a lively shop in our village, on Water Street, named Windswept Dreams. She tells me that at night she adds two drops of vanilla extract to her rose-hip tea. Later I learned that vanilla helps insomniacs. Vanilla is appealing because our body associates it with sugar and fat. When we eat, our opiate levels rise, and we feel good.

It is possible to take a more active role in our wellness by adding some of these natural ingredients to our tea, not necessarily to soothe our aches and pains, but because it pleases our senses. I'd take jasmine over cod-liver oil, wouldn't you? We don't have to wait to be told by some "authority" that it's all right to throw a slice of green apple in our tea, or stir it with a cinnamon stick, or dip our ginger snap in our herbal tea. Smells that comfort us and evoke cozy memories add to the mystical experience of tea. Bulgari's Eau Parfumée smells like green tea. A sensory psychologist once commented that if someone smells delicious, like food, you want them near you.

There are too many conventional tea rules. Should we use lemon? Should we use milk and sugar? Is cream allowed? William James admonishes us that truth is what works. You and only you know how you want your tea flavored tonight, tomorrow, and the next day. Not only are you free to choose, but you can be innovative and open to new ways to enhance your feeling of relaxation, comfort, and awareness.

The scent of tea permeates your house, and it makes you feel good. Like perfume that you associate with pleasant memories, the remembrance of the smells

The whole of life lies in the verb seeing.

PIERRE TEILHARD DE CHARDIN

from your mother's kitchen when you were a child is comforting. Last fall our house was on a kitchen tour for a local charity. On the stove, we simmered apples, oranges, cinnamon sticks, and some herbal teas. In the oven, we baked chocolate-chip cookies.

While people were looking around, they seemed glad to be there. At the end of the day, several visitors came back for another look around and to absorb the smell of our house. One curious woman wanted a recipe for my concoction. Flattered, I let her inhale the perfumed steam for a time, and then I asked her to guess. "Tea, ahh, I smell tea." I'd thrown in several different tea bags and some herbs, and had also added fruit. Of course, I could have used loose tea as well. Unlike the tea you drink, this concoction can be reheated a number of times, adding more water, apples, cinnamon, and tea. Try peach and mandarin orange—it is a delicious combination. Our whole house absorbs the smells. I love to sit upstairs in bed and breathe in the happiness emanating from our kitchen stove.

Tea is part of a continuum of human experience. Like reading ancient wisdom in hopes some of it will rub off on us, we sip tea knowing that we are in the company of truth seekers who practiced this ritual centuries before Christ. We are participating in a ceremony full of powerful associations that can have beneficial physiological consequences for us if we are but aware of them. We can use tea to infuse our soul with more sacredness. Tea can symbolize an expanded, open mind. It can be an invitation to participate in a celebration of life that connects us to universal form and beauty. In a certain sense, tea can gently guide us on our path. And whenever we feel empowered spiritually, we expand our consciousness. Paracelsus, an ancient Greek poet, reminds us of the need to develop our whole personality:

> He who knows nothing, loves nothing. He who can do nothing, understands nothing. He who understands nothing is worthless. But he who understands also loves, notices, sees. . . . The more knowledge is inherent in a thing, the greater the love. . . . Anyone who imagines that all fruits ripen at the same time as the strawberries knows nothing about grapes.

Tea helps a soul to ripen. Serenity and contentment are the result of this transformed awareness. If you've never properly treated yourself to a tea for one, I urge you to issue an invitation to yourself today. Take out your favorite cup and saucer; lovingly choose your best-loved teapot and water pitcher; choose an agreeable span of time; breathe deeply and look forward to your own company.

Chapter IV

TEA

FOR

TWO

How do we become true and good, happy and genuine, joyful and free? Never by magic, never by chance, never by sitting and waiting, but only by getting in touch with good, true, happy, genuine human beings, only by seeking the company of the strong and the free, only by catching spontaneity and freedom from those who are themselves spontaneous and free.

—CHARLES MALIK

The tea ceremony naturally evolves from one of solitude to one of companionship, genuine relatedness, acceptance, and approval.

The difference between the solo and the twosome is interaction—conversation with another person. Here, we pay attention to a fellow human being in an atmosphere and environment of understanding. We face each other openly. We come together consensually because we value being able to share mutual appreciation and affection. Those of whom we are most fond, we come to see as our other half. We bring the same focus, concentration, and honesty to this mutual experience as we do to the occasion of tea for one.

The atmosphere of intimacy surrounding the tea ritual allows us to get in close touch with our own nature as well as becoming more aware of someone else. We look into the eyes of a trusted human soul. Anything can happen when we don't try to force things but come to the encounter open to the moments as they reveal themselves to us. The circumstances of the moment will provide spontaneity and insights that will refresh us, delight us, and amuse us if we only let that happen.

Richard Baker, writing the introduction to *Zen Mind, Beginner's Mind* by Shunryu Suzuki, suggests that the Zen master "takes the most difficult but persuasive way to talk about Buddhism—in terms of the ordinary circumstances of people's lives—to try to convey the whole of the teaching in statements as simple as 'Have a cup of tea.'" In a hurried age when everyone is overstressed,

The first cup moistens my lips . . . The second cup breaks my loneliness The third cup searches my barren entrail The fourth cup raises a slight perspiration The fifth cup purifies me The sixth cup calls me to the realm of the immortals The seventh . . . I can take no more.

CHINESE POET, UNKNOWN

conflicted, and in need of soothing, tea can restore us to equilibrium. An important element in the tea ritual is that it be nonthreatening, nonconfrontational. Tea is not lunch or even breakfast; it is not an occasion for the transaction of business, for the making of deals. Tea is for getting acquainted, for cementing friendships, for the accepting and giving of pleasure.

Because tea is my time to listen to myself, when I ask someone to join me for tea, I want to listen to that person's story. Each interchange is different. Honoring another person requires concentra-

tion. I am not only stimulated by this intensity, but I am totally absorbed in what's going on. When you want to catch up with someone you haven't seen for a while, tea is ideal. There is nothing that keeps you from each other. When you try to have this same connection over a meal at your house, the flow of the conversation is interrupted by the necessity of having to jump up to remove plates and clear the table. Similarly, if you are in a restaurant, the spell is so often broken with the waiter's refrain, "Is everything all right?" Each interruption makes it difficult

to regain the closeness that was there before the intrusion.

Every ceremony has its own chemistry. I've observed that when two people share this ritual, not only are they attentive, but they sit calmly and speak slowly and quietly. We move with grace because this special encounter relaxes us. Usually we invite a friend over for tea in the late afternoon, when the hassles of the day are behind us. No matter how busy our lives are at work, tea slows down our tempo. Do, do, do. Go, go, go. Pop in here. Call. Meet. Greet. Join. Lunch. Talk, argue, analyze, compromise. The high-gear pace many of us live with creates the feeling that enough is never enough and that the desk can never be cleared. Tea reminds us that enough *is* enough, and that to know what work is, we must know relaxation as well.

Tea isn't result-oriented; it is a process. There should be no set agenda, no goals or expectations. By *being* right there, you slowly unwind into your real rhythm. This is an extremely sensuous feeling. You are no longer in conflict; therefore you become more subtle and graceful in the ways you express yourself. No longer projected into the future waiting for a more important event, we learn to live in the moment. Maybe the closest we'll ever get to becoming a sage is now, as we focus attention away from ourselves to another. Self-consciousness is forgotten as soul meets soul in reverence and affection.

Until the past ten or so years, I mostly had tea with people older than I am. I remember back in 1947 having tea in the garden of the rectory with my grandfather. It was the year before he died. He hadn't removed his clerical collar as he often did Sunday afternoon, and he leaned forward in his chair to get closer to me. Grandfather Johns made me feel utterly loved and important. For him, even as a child I was a person worthy of his attention. The tea ceremony was an excuse to be together.

The meaning of life is found in openness to being and "being present" in full awareness.
THOMAS MERTON

My godmother, Mitzi Christian, also loved the tea ritual. She and Mother had tea regularly. They got so involved in conversation that once Mitzi's daughter, Anne, waited for nearly an hour—that seemed like a century to a small child—before she could catch her mother's eye. I recall Anne telling me, "Your mother is a really good talker!"

Whenever Mitzi had tea with me alone, which was often, she never patronized me, never treated me like a child. She was an artist and an art historian. She was wise, beautiful, and full of grace. Because she took me seriously, she made me feel that it was possible for me to fulfill my potential.

Tea is anything but casual. Our eyes, tone of voice, the nuances of our facial expression, our body language, reveal us. There are no distractions when we have this face-to-face encounter; deceptions are not possible. We become ageless, joined together in the mystery. All these older women, including my art teacher and dear Eleanor McMillen Brown, gave of themselves and offered glimpses into grown-up life. They didn't act with condescension toward this awkward kid with dirt under her fingernails. Rather, they took an interest

If you cannot find the truth right where you are, where else do you expect to find it?

DOGEN

90

in me and made me feel valuable. With each tea ceremony, the grown-up world unfolded before me, and I began to see what the future had in store.

These tea times for two have constituted a continuum in my life. Without conscious thought, I, too, am now having tea "with the young," as Eleanor Brown would say with affection, and a flick of her delicate hand.

When you are the younger person in a relationship, you may worry whether you're really welcome, and whether you're wasting the precious time of an older, wiser  adult. I used to question my importance in the eyes of these revered people whom I held in such high esteem. I was concerned that I couldn't offer enough in return for what they were so selflessly giving me. By accepting me, they made me believe in myself and my growth and made me immensely happy. Whenever we are happy, we transcend ourselves. A metamorphosis takes place. Our mind expands, and we are able to experience the gifts the moment presents. We lose some of our old ways and thoughts and begin to glimpse new possibilities.

Tea breaks down barriers of age, sex, background, and status. Once we are together, sipping tea, a new way of experiencing the world opens up. We set aside, at least momentarily, past disappointments and concerns about the future and become present to the person who is with us. These older role models taught me discipline and generosity. By offering me unqualified love, these women and men

 enhanced my worth. Magnanimous people have no vanity, jealousy, or pettiness, and therefore are able to share of themselves freely.

When we are celebrating a special time together, over tea, we learn about ourselves, about our talent for friendship, about our capacity for closeness and companionship. Rather than feeling we can't make a difference, we become suffused with well-being, which in turn gives us enormous hope. We feel connected to the past and excited about the future as we enjoy the present. I realized only recently how deeply I have been influenced by these one-on-one teas I had with older people.

Now that I am older, I relish the opportunity of inviting a younger person to tea and learning about the person's interests, loves, and losses. Much support can be shared over tea when people get together for the sole purpose of being there for each other. We are told that placebos work their "magic" one third of the time. If tea seems to have similar magical properties, then why not give the leaves the credit they deserve?

Having tea with another person requires a commitment. The most precious resource we have is time. When we want to be with another person enough to not have anything

We are here and it is now.

H. L. MENCKEN

or anyone else interfere, we are putting intention into action. Tea cannot be just a metaphor. Tea must be experienced. The men, women, and children whom we hold in high regard are all potential teaists to us.

While I'm realistic enough to know that we cannot have tea with every interesting person we meet, when we do have tea with someone, we will find our soul lifted, and we will feel wiser. Wherever we are, we will feel we are in the right place. Tea gives us the opportunity for confirmation and affirmation.

Very little is needed to make a happy life.
MARCUS AURELIUS

Most of the older people I used to have tea with have died. Our celebrations are over, but the memories and their impact on me linger. Fortunately, our lives overlapped. I now know with certainty that these shared moments were as special to the people I looked up to so highly as they were to me. One can always sense when love is there.

It is perfectly appropriate to invite yourself to have tea with someone elderly who can no longer get around much or who may be housebound. If you make this a weekly ritual, you'll probably find that you'll actually come to look forward to these visits as much as the elderly person and that both of you will come away stimulated and enriched.

When I had tea with Mrs. Brown, we often talked about decorating. I'd tell her about my jobs, and she very much enjoyed visualizing the rooms I described to her in great detail. When I described to her that I was using quilts on the walls of a bank in lieu of paintings, her eyes smiled in delight.

When you call to invite yourself for a visit over tea with an older friend, give them a choice of dates. This is respectful, and it makes the person feel special. Make your date a week or so ahead to enhance the sense of anticipation. Always bring a little something gift-wrapped. We never outgrow our love for presents. After the tea, send a thank-you note. Elderly people appreciate these formal gestures, and they cherish being remembered.

A midafternoon recently, my assistant, Elisabeth, and I were literally dragging our feet. We'd been going from meeting to meeting. Each of us carried tote bags that seemed heavier as the hours went by. We were a block away from Felissimo, just west of Fifth Avenue at Fifty-sixth Street. We knew that on the fourth floor of that store there is a wonderful tearoom that we could take refuge in, sit down, sip tea, and calm our minds and bodies. The very anticipation lightened our loads as we moved toward our destination.

The elevator was crowded, and we decided to use the stairs. Sore feet aside, I always prefer stairs to elevators. That

very morning I read Dr. Deepak Chopra's wonderful book *Ageless Body, Timeless Mind.* In it, he stresses the importance of taking responsibility for our own lives. He tells of a Parisian doctor who wrote about longevity and who himself lived to be 103. He "arose to work on his book at age ninety-nine, he reached his study by climbing three flights of stairs." It is I who felt like a ninety-nine-year-old as I climbed the spiral staircase to the tearoom. But as I began anticipating the taste of tea, my gait got lighter and quicker. We stopped on each floor to look at the exhibitions of the Zenue lifestyle, which "embodies simplicity, the earth and the elements . . . a life in harmony with nature, a feeling of balance, a moment of clarity. Zenue rediscovers the past and re-imagines the future." On one of the floors, we were handed a brochure that invited us to discover and explore this Zenue lifestyle that "invigorates the senses and relaxes the mind." When we arrived on the fourth floor, we looked at a display of Japanese tableware so stunningly arranged that the subtle beauty of each piece from sake cups to teacups, bowls, and even chopsticks was brought into relief.

When we got to the tearoom, we were asked by the hostess where we wanted to sit. We selected a small oval table, dropped our packages, and eased our weary bodies into chairs. "You're welcome to smell the teas. We have thirty-seven different varieties," the waitress said. We began with the black teas, the black blended teas, and the green teas. Elisabeth and I loved the smell of Jasmine Jazz, which the tin label calls a "romance enhancer." "Rarest Jasmine Blossom Green Tea. A perfect balancer to strong tasting foods, sweet green leaves mate with fragrant blossoms to make this Yin Kao Jasmine the world's finest." Leave it to us to be attracted to the most expensive tea in the entire selection! We moved on to sniff the herbal teas; we particularly liked the Lemon Wintermint, the Orange Ginger Mint, and Cocoa Carob Mint. They are caffeine-free, however, and we wanted a perk-up.

Perhaps there is nothing to figure out after all: perhaps we only need to wake up.

THOMAS MERTON

The waitress informed us that all the teas were served in teapots at the same price. Of course, the store sells all the teas on the menu, and you can buy reusable tins. Each tin contains enough to make approximately sixty cups. We decided to share a large pot of Jasmine Jazz, and to make the experience even more perfect, we also ordered Jasmine tea ice cream! When the waitress brought our tea on a

teakwood slab tray in a black pot, she put down a glass dish, which we assumed contained our ice cream. Famished and tired, we both dived into it at the same time, discovering, to our surprise, that it was honey—organic honey at that.

It wasn't exactly ice cream, but it was so good that we both licked our spoons. It's true, isn't it, that eating sugar raises the opiate levels in the brain, making us feel good?

We sipped our tea and felt renewed. Elisabeth suggested that all the people who worked in the neighborhood should go to Felissimo for a tea break. It would give them a chance to regroup spiritually, she said, and then be much more productive.

The Republic of Tea has a saying, "There is nothing that cannot be lost, no problem that will not disappear, no burden that will not float away, between the first sip and the last."

Our Jasmine tea ice cream arrived, and we were told that the *osen bei* organic cookie stuck in the top was pineapple-flavored. The tea and ice cream suffused us with good feelings toward each other and the world.

Our waitress told us we could keep the three-inch-long birch twigs enclosed in our napkins as mementos of our special afternoon.

Walking down the four flights of marble stairs, we felt reborn. Finding ourselves once more in the bustle of New York's crowded streets, we both began to laugh. Our tea celebration lasted two hours, and we were late for our five o'clock meeting uptown. While immersed in the Japanese tea ceremony, we lost all sense of time, an all-too-rare happening for all of us who live by the clock.

Everyone around us seemed to be in an acute state of distress. Jostled and bumped, we nonetheless felt a joy that no one could take away from us. We were temporarily realigned, centered.

Miraculously, we found a vacant taxi. We climbed in and glided uptown, arriving before our clients, who had been delayed in a meeting downtown. We gave them some Black Currant and Earl Grey iced tea laced with freshly squeezed orange juice and crushed mint. I enjoyed watching them as they melted into the upholstery, breathed more easily, and sipped the refreshing brew.

One of the most beneficial rewards of the tea celebration is that it enriches the rest of the day. Whenever I hear the "Ode to Joy" ("Joyful, joyful, we adore thee") in Beethoven's Ninth Symphony, there is a residual grace that stays with me through all the activities that follow. That night, before going to sleep, I wondered if we, too, wouldn't have stayed caught up in the hurried hassle if we hadn't offered ourselves a true respite?

To sensible men, every day is a day of reckoning.
JOHN W. GARDNER

If we become so transformed by the tea ritual every time we participate in it, what can we learn from this experience? We begin to understand that it is not so much the kind of tea you drink but the peace that it brings you. You feel the warmth, the companionship and love, not just of the other person but of humanity. It's amazing to me that something so modest and simple as tea has such power in the expansion of one's consciousness.

I think of the artist Robert Henri, a dedicated teacher, whose intelligent and practical guide, *The Art Spirit,* is read in art schools:

I'm not young enough to know everything.

J. M. BARRIE

> There are moments in our lives, there are moments in a day, when we seem to see beyond the usual. Such are the moments of our greatest happiness. Such are the moments of our greatest wisdom. . . . If one could but recall his vision by some sort of sign. It was in this hope that the arts were invented. Sign-posts on the way to what may be. Sign-posts toward greater knowledge.

We all know, at least intuitively, that there is a close relationship between art and life. In fact, the definition of an artist is someone who is in constant touch with his true nature. Tea allows each one of us to feel as free as an artist, free in the sense of expressing our own spirit. Tea for two encourages the opening of our self to another self. The right environment has that effect on us. Tea, under the right circumstances, is where you are most *you*. At a tea for two, you are removed from distractions; you come together with another person in order to focus on them. You become one with your surroundings and clear your mind.

When the pace of your life is out of control, without your being aware of it, your very voice acquires another pitch. You sound "off." You make too many plans, you have too many goals, you go to too many places, you literally *process* too many people. This "you" is not going to be able to participate in the tea ritual for two because it won't seem like a big enough "deal," and not worth the time. Tea for two must become a priority, a time to forget yourself. If you let it become a priority, you will realize that the time you take for tranquil communication will result in clearer vision. You will be surprised to discover yourself able to accomplish more in shorter periods of time.

> *Your life is the sum of your present moments, so if you're missing lots of them, you may actually miss much of your children's infancy and youth, or beautiful sunsets, or the beauty of your own body.*
> DR. JON KABAT-ZINN

Tea for two is a mutual invitation for honesty and openness. Only *you* can bring meaning to the ceremony and turn it into a memorable experience. This is all there is to it; it's that simple. If you are already at peace, you will feel even more secure, and if you are anxious, you will find the environment conducive to a calm evaluation of your present reality. Use this time to commune with your host or guest and seek advice and comfort if you need it.

Tea for two is nonjudgmental. I know this from the experience of having tea with older, wiser people of accomplishment. All I could bring to the celebration was myself. But isn't that all we can ever bring to any experience? We should never be embarrassed by who we are, or the hand that is dealt us. Be proud of who you are, and give yourself the right to take pleasure in yourself and those around you.

Most people think of tea as a sharing ritual. Those of us who create our own solitude don't often discuss it. It seems almost impolite to describe in glowing language the experience of being alone,

calm and still. For the ceremony to be all it can be, there has to be a conviction of the value of this activity, not only to us, but to others. But it doesn't really matter whether you are alone and quiet or engaged in intense intimacy with an older or younger person. When you are open to tea, you gain strength from the ritual. Man, woman, child, old, young, healthy, ill, happy, sad, inspired or depressed, hopeful or discouraged, everyone can benefit from this experience. You honor life with tea, and the only way you can do this is by making the effort to stop time.

"Living," as wise Eleanor Brown once said, "takes time." Even though she died January 30, 1991, a little over a week before her 101st birthday, Mrs. Brown is alive in my heart. I never saw her rushed or anxious. She was an interior designer working for prominent families in America, and there were many times when clients tried to put undue pressure on her and her staff. This was unacceptable to her. She valued everything about her life and didn't want discord or manipulation.

At four o'clock every weekday afternoon, a maid served tea to Mrs. Brown and to all the employees. Cookies, too. No matter how frantic we were, or upset or stressed, we all stopped working. Tea was a command performance with Mrs. Brown. This was a time for sharing. I switched my attitude instantly. She'd engage me in questions. "What was the most beautiful thing you saw today? Why?" Or, "Don't you feel we get too fussy in our decorations?" Or, "Did you know our client Mrs. Harris is home *every* afternoon when her daughters return from school, and they have tea together?"

I learned that teaching is in the act, in the performance. What you do, you are. Our four o'clock teas at the firm were not four-hour Japanese tea ceremonies, but they did happen every day. Probably they lasted twenty minutes, which is one hundred minutes a week. This adds up. In a year, you have had 5,200 minutes of tea, or a little over 86 hours. Think of what you and someone else can share in that time.

> When you understand one thing through and through, you understand everything.
> SHUNRYU SUZUKI

Mrs. Brown was an extremely successful

businesswoman. Why did she instigate this ceremony in 1922, when she founded her firm, and serve tea for over sixty years, every afternoon, to her employees? It forced us to stop whatever we were doing and pause. Over tea we dreamed up solutions to design projects. We tended to pair up. A younger assistant could spend some one-on-one time with her boss or a senior designer. Of all the habits I've acquired from Mrs. Brown, my adopting the tea ceremony at four each afternoon at Alexandra Stoddard Incorporated is one for which I'm especially grateful. This break refreshes us and clears our heads.

When my assistant, Elisabeth, and I sit alone having tea, we talk about our work in broad, speculative terms. We talk about the big picture and let go of pressing problems for a time. Sitting at a desk isn't the only time when ideas surface; in fact, it is much more likely that something new springs to mind in moments of peace and leisure.

I have several very busy friends who enjoy coming over for tea after work before going home to their families. The more frenzied we become, the more important it is to take undiluted time to be with a friend. Peter also enjoys having tea with friends or a grandchild. He likes to sit in the living room or library, whereas I take a friend to our bedroom because it is quiet; there's a door to shut and a gracious sitting area with a tea table, chairs, and a small sofa. The paintings, the colors, and the airy atmosphere—everything is soft, warm, and com-

This is my way.
What is your way?
The way doesn't exist.

FRIEDRICH NIETZSCHE

forting. I set up the tea tray ahead of time, so that when the doorbell rings, I steep the tea, and in five minutes we're pouring our first cup.

I am always flattered when a friend calls me on the spur of the moment and asks if she can come by for tea. But if I have tea plans, I make another date. Tea for two is a special opportunity to catch up and talk in shorthand and get to the marrow of life.

A third party, no matter who it is, changes the chemistry and can be an unwelcome intrusion. There are far too few occasions when two people are alone, face-to-face, in communion with one another. Each meeting should be sacrosanct, even if it is only for twenty minutes. Just being together, sometimes even without a whole lot of conversation, binds us with invisible threads of grace and love.

Both people yield to a shared moment of peace. We find happiness because we took time. Nothing else matters, because for a few sacred minutes we wash away our cares as we sit calmly holding a teacup and saucer. The sides of our mouths curl up in pure delight. "Aahh. Mmmm." The magic spell never fails.

None of us will ever know the impact we may have on another soul. And I'm not at all certain it matters whether we know. It is important to give unqualified love to someone who needs us. We ought to share our positive attitude, energy, and spirit. It shouldn't be a burden to listen if someone we care about wants to express her feelings or ask our advice. Over tea, the mind stops racing and focuses.

> With all of your science, can you tell how ...light comes into the soul?
>
> HENRY DAVID THOREAU

When I was in Indianapolis for a lecture, I mentioned to my audience my tea book-in-progress. At the luncheon, a most attractive woman shared with me a wonderful anecdote, and I asked her to write it down for me. The letter that follows tells this delightful tea story in Cynthia's own words:

Dear Ms. Stoddard,

It was so nice to meet you at the elegant Country Luncheon for the Connor Prairie Alliance. You and your delightful husband were a ray of sunshine on a blustery day.

At your request I am writing to tell the story of how I got my red-haired twins:

In 1974, on a chilly March afternoon, I was a guest in the home of my friend, Jill Bower. Jill is a native of Broadstairs, County of Kent, in England. Even though she had lived in the United States several years she continued to observe the English custom of having afternoon tea. It was my pleasure to be her frequent guest. She would mention from time to time that only one person is allowed to touch the tea pot. Once a person is designated to pour the tea it is bad luck for anyone else to pour after that. Anyone who disregards this warning will give birth to ginger twins. [Translate that into red-haired twins.]

I had always heeded this warning, but on this particular afternoon I backslid. We were enjoying the tea that Jill had poured when she left the room briefly to tend to her baby. In her absence I poured myself another cup. When she returned and saw what I had done she good-naturedly said I would be sorry, reminding me of the ginger twins. That's just a silly superstition, I said. On March 10, 1975, I gave birth to twin boys with hair the color of a new penny. Jill was highly amused.

I would like to dispel any thought that having ginger twins is bad luck. No one on earth feels more fortunate than my husband and I. Cory and Gabriel, now eighteen, continue to be a joy and a blessing.

Sincerely,
Cynthia Fisher

Who knows? You could have tea for two also and end up with ginger twins. It's all a wonderful mystery.

Chapter V

TEA
PARTIES

There are few hours in life more agreeable
than the hour dedicated to the ceremony
known as afternoon tea.

—HENRY JAMES

The closeness and intimacy we share sipping tea for two is vastly different from the atmosphere of a tea party. Tea parties often have a wedding-reception feel to them; people dress up, women sometimes even wear colorful hats, and light conversation prevails and is a welcome respite from the seriousness of much of daily life.

Tea celebrations provide a sense of community. We are invited to participate in a special event. Sometimes there is music and dancing, most often to the nostalgic tunes of Lester Lanin or the sounds of Bob Hardwick. Delicious finger sandwiches of watercress, cucumber, tomato, sliced egg, and cream cheese and walnuts are passed on doily-lined trays decorated with parsley and flowers. Nothing overpowers the subtle scent of the tea, the perfume in the air, and the memories brought to life by the music of our youth.

We see our friends' children and ask questions about their lives. We meet acquaintances and inquire about their interests and accomplishments as well as those of their children. Tea parties are just nice.

If you get simple beauty and nought else; You get about the best thing God invents.

ROBERT BROWNING

In 1959, my parents presented me to their friends at a tea at our house in Westport, Connecticut. The local photographer was hired. Both his sons, twins, were in my class at Staples High School and attended the tea. My hair was combed in a page boy, held in perfect place, I recall, by Elizabeth Arden's Blue Grass hair spray. My ice-blue taffeta dress was tied at the waist with a wide velvet sash in a richer French blue. Of course, my shoes were "dyed to match" the sash.

Mother loved to give teas and did so with regularity. She usually would do so on Saturday afternoons. One can just imagine the men groaning at having to leave the golf course, the fishing boat, or the tennis game early to go home, clean up, don the "perfect" necktie-and-shirt combination, and be ready to drive to the tea "on time."

Whether they came there forcibly or not, everyone did seem to have a good time. One of my mother's best friends was a passionate gardener. She always arrived wearing white gloves because her hands were permanently stained with the good earth.

Mother never had her tea parties catered. The food was always prepared at home. I still have my first cookbook, *Kitchen Fun,* which was given to me when I was a little girl. It is full of food stains and memories. When I was just five, Mother taught me how to roll a watercress sandwich. The trick is to use a rolling pin on thinly sliced day-old white Pepperidge Farm bread. Margaret (Maggie) Rudkin, who founded the successful bread company named after her nearby farm, was a friend of my parents .

Whatever interests, is interesting.
WILLIAM HAZLITT

Mr. Rudkin was not in good health, so Mrs. Rudkin would bake bread and sweets to try to strengthen him. Of course, friends would be offered samples. When the Rudkins came to dinner at our old onion farm on Compo Parkway in Westport, Connecticut, they would never arrive empty-handed. In a calico-lined basket, Mrs. Rudkin would give Mother three or four different kinds of loaves. Pepperidge Farm is to this day one of America's great success stories. When I was a child, our class would go watch the bread-making. The smell of the kitchen still lingers with me. I recall that at the end of the visit, each of us was given a hot, freshly baked loaf to take home. You can imagine how much of that loaf ever got to the kitchen table after our bus ride back to school. Recently, I retraced my steps to the Pepperidge Farm. Al Silva, the plant manager, arranged for me to revisit the bakery. I was very moved by the visit, to be in the same bakery and to smell the molasses, the cinnamon, and the wheat just as I had when I was a little girl.

He who knows others is wise; He who knows himself is enlightened.

TAO-TE CHING

Mother knew how to make a good sandwich. After we rolled the Pepperidge Farm bread, we coated it lightly with soft sweet butter, then spread a fine layer of Hellmann's mayonnaise over the butter, fresh-ground white pepper, and watercress. We put a sprig of watercress on each side of the bread with the leaves hanging outside, anchored in place by the stems the length of the bread. Rolling away from us, we made each one a masterpiece. We put them on platters and cov-  ered them with waxed paper and then a slightly damp dish towel. Mother's watercress sandwiches never broke apart, were never held together with a toothpick, and were never soggy. She was like a Zen master in the kitchen. Utter concentration was required. She'd get me to care about the consequences of sloppy work by saying, "You wouldn't want Miss Arden to spill on her dress and have it leave a dark mayonnaise stain, would you, dear?" My father was vice president of Elizabeth Arden for several years, and Miss Arden would come out from New York City to visit a number of times, especially on the occasion of Mother's tea parties.

Another favorite I loved to make were sliced cucumber hearts. I had a set of cookie cutters, and Mother would measure the diameter of the cucum-

ber to make sure it was large enough for a heart. We
worked as a team. Mother peeled the cucumbers

and scored or sculpted them with
a dinner fork. (This brings out the
flavor and looks quite pretty.) I
would then use the cookie cutter.
The hearts were one eighth inch
thick. The ones that weren't big
enough to make hearts we'd shape
with a round cookie cutter. All the scraps were saved
for bread pudding.

Everything was pleasing to the eye, since our
goal was to bring grace and gentility to the moment.
If a sandwich was open-faced, there would be a decoration in the center. The tops of the hearts were
dipped with paprika. How long has it been since
you've used paprika?

A tomato would be cut with a sharp German
paring knife into petals that made it look like a rose.
White and red radishes were turned into flowers or
sliced paper-thin and used as garnish on sandwiches.
It was during the preparation for these tea parties
that I began to understand how much pleasure these
events brought to my mother. She loved every last

detail, from polishing the silver tray and tea service to putting out the sugar cubes. She liked putting cloves in the lemon slices and arranging flowers on beautiful platters.

Mother truly enjoyed the orchestration of these teas, and I'm the richer for having been her helper. It was at these moments that she shed her parental role and acted almost like a doting grandmother, simply delighting in our companionship. I was eager to learn in the kitchen, and we both had fun. Long before the party began, she shed her cares. Because I have memories of her in less tranquil moods, I treasure the memory of these tea parties, where she was serene and was able to draw satisfaction from the moment.

Whether she and I sat at the breakfast-room table or if she brought me a tray in bed when I was sick, she always put a plate under the tea saucer as an unnecessary—and therefore all the more elegant—touch. This was her signature. It made tea a bigger deal. It turned out to be also practical, because if someone bumped into you, the tea would

> The finest kind of friendship is between people who expect a great deal of each other but never ask it.
>
> SYLVIA BREMER

cascade onto the second plate. Cookies, sweet cakes, scones with jam—all had a place to go.

Each cup of tea represents an imaginary voyage.
CATHERINE DOUZEL

She would place a linen or cotton napkin on top of a pretty dessert plate and then would serve tea and put the cup and saucer on the napkin. Even if someone never removed the plate, the presentation was attractive, and the saucer didn't slide around. At large tea parties, there isn't always a place at a table for each guest, so the extra plate improvises as a stand-up place setting.

Can you remember some of your favorite tea parties of long ago? On Sundays in Northampton, Massachusetts, where I went to an all-girls boarding school, we were allowed to have visitors for tea, which was presided over by our very proper headmistress, Miss Peters. Our dates had to wear coat and tie and were subjected to grilling by the stern matriarch. Only the "good young men" (whatever that meant) were allowed to walk with us after tea on the designated walking path. No matter how miserable and impatient the boy, she would coax him into talking about his junior year at Deerfield, his classes, his plans for college, and the football team. We were all in the same boat, trying to eat the fruit-cake, avoiding the candied fruit. We'd cast furtive glances at the grandfather clock, wondering how five minutes could feel like a whole semester.

One of my callers, a teacher of English at Williams College, had no interest in going on the walking path with me. He actually enjoyed tea with Miss Peters, and her mother, Mrs. Emerson, the school's founder, and me. I could barely grasp what they were talking about, and yet I was drawn into the conversation enthusiastically. Tall, handsome Dee Gardner and I had met at a wedding. He was older than I and liked to check up on me from time to time. Our parents were friends, and we share god-parents. Mrs. Emerson was in her late seventies and had a soft, round face with a sweet, ready smile. She often led chapel, and I liked how she expressed herself. Looking back, Dee's serious interest in my education was endearing. He cross-examined Mrs. Emerson and Mrs. Peters, which forced them to formulate their vision of education for us girls. All this sounded

Every day is
a good day.
YUN-MEN

important, and I was offered an unexpected chance to appreciate the school's goals.

Tea parties bring back childhood memories and other anecdotes relating to tea. Jacques Barzun, in his book *A Stroll with William James,* tells us that when William James was teaching at Harvard, he and his wife would invite students for tea. James would make a point of looking out for the shy ones and drawing them into conversation with him.

Tea parties are part of our collective consciousness. My editor Rose Marie Morse remembers that as a child in Yugoslavia she was taken to her aunt's house for afternoon tea. Friends were invited and encouraged to drop in. This was a daily ritual, not an occasional happening to mark a coming-of-age or to honor a special event like an engagement or birthday. Around five o'clock, friends would come to share in conversation and hear stories laced with gossip. On the tea tray, one found milk, lemon slices, sugar, and a small cut-crystal decanter of dark rum. In winter a dash of rum must have hit the spot. I'm sure the English put a splash of rum in tea to ease the chill of drafty houses.

> For everything that
> lives is holy;
> life delights in life.
> WILLIAM BLAKE

This tea took place at a time when women often had household help, and few worked outside the house. Tea was a wonderful way to exchange news and insights, discuss literature and the latest museum exhibit. This usually took place before men returned home from work. But now, with computers, faxes, photocopying machines, and answering machines, men are working more from home  and gladly join in afternoon tea, sometimes inviting over their own friends as well.

If you are an artist or a writer and work alone most of the day, tea is an ideal time to be convivial, to walk away from your work and be grateful for the break. If you have well-informed friends, isn't it fun to have a lively exchange with them about politics and world events? I think so. Rather than absorb information passively, we can enter into stimulating dialogue. Discussing history or the influence of art and music on society while sipping strong black tea can be a heady experience.

Everywhere my aunt and I went on our world tour, we were introduced to different cultures and lifestyles. It now seems extraordinary, but back in 1959 we went to several tea parties a day. It was here we learned about local customs, decoration, tastes, style, and dress as well as values and beliefs. Whether at an embassy or at the home of a poor family, we were served beautifully. If everyone could go around the world sipping tea with people in their homes, what a profound effect it would have on our educations!

People who genuinely wished to honor us in this way became very special and memorable to us. If the black tea was too strong for my taste, as it was in Ceylon (now Sri Lanka), I would water it down, add milk and sugar. But I quickly got the real message of tea. It was the vehicle that provided the focus for the visit.

There are many wonderful, useful tea books at the library or in bookstores. You can find recipes for scones, biscuits, cookies, and finger sandwiches in your favorite cookbooks or file boxes that you have filled with recipes passed on from family and friends. Those of you who bake know how to make scones. When the blueberries are sweet and plump, you feel compelled to pop them in some sugary dough and put them in a greased muffin tin. Sometimes I get the urge to make lemon sugar cookies. But there are other times, most times, when I open a tin of Crabtree & Evelyn lemon cookies and know theirs are better than mine.

I don't think it is important that you do your own baking or that you rack your brain to find exotic ways of serving tea. Tea should not be an occasion for anxiety. As it stands, it is a ceremony rich in tradition; all you need to do is add your own touches to make the most of the moment. While it's fun to imitate how others serve tea, the occasion is enriched when we create our own small customs.

A friend is a present you give yourself.

ROBERT LOUIS STEVENSON

Just as a friend is a gift we give ourselves, so is tea. It is good to turn our attention to beauty and ritual and grace. It is a form of thanksgiving to plan ahead and invite friends to a tea party. Paradoxically, the event is both simple and sophisticated. People meet at teas and become friends, even lovers!

We have to remind ourselves to be who we are. Tea parties are no exception. In 1979, when my mother was diagnosed with terminal cancer and had only a few months to live, I gave a tea party in her honor. I invited all my closest friends to celebrate her, to honor her. When our emotions are in turmoil, we tend to overdo. Her advice on this occasion, as on so many others, rang true. "Darling, just do what you like to do; the tea party will be beautiful." Her advice was reassuring, and I got busy with the plans.

For all serious daring
starts from within.

EUDORA WELTY

The tea was scheduled for six o'clock, because most of my friends work and some had to travel some distance to attend. I figured if I didn't want to eat sticky-sweet things at that hour, my friends wouldn't either. I served scrumptious and attractive open-faced sandwiches. For the tea, I chose a blend of black Earl Grey and Orange Spice, and that was just right. People love to taste something different from what they ordinarily have at home.

That night, there was a wonderful feeling of warmth in our apartment. I never wanted the fire to go out. Several friends were so touched by the occasion that they arranged teas of their own. We all met once a month for a year. We came together to stay in touch and share our thoughts and latest news. Each tea party had its own dynamics, and we all showed up enthusiastically. After a while, people moved, became busier, and we stopped having these lovely get-togethers.

The tea party is a spa for the soul. You leave your cares and work behind. Busy people forget their business. Your stress melts away, your senses awaken, and you make time to be loving with yourself.

Tea parties are not as noisy as cocktail parties. Liquor tends to make people speak louder. At a tea party, usually there are more areas where you can sit and sip your tea in quiet conversation. A cocktail party is always more of a scene. You say hello, but it's often hard to really talk with any one person. At a tea, you might sit for as long as thirty minutes with one or two people and somehow create your own mini-party.

Several years ago in Albuquerque when I was on a book tour, a friend gave a tea in my honor. If Sue had organized the tea at her ranch, not everyone

We think in generalities; but we live in detail.
ALFRED NORTH WHITEHEAD

would have had the time to drive the eighteen miles out of town to her house. Sue and a group of friends came up with the idea of having the tea at the quaint mall where I was lecturing and signing books. There was a storefront for rent, and they were able to charm the real estate agent into borrowing the space for the occasion.

They magically turned this vacant space into *The Tea House.* Each sixty-inch round folding table was decorated by a different person with a tablecloth, napkins, teacups and saucers, teapots and flower vases and cookie dishes all brought from the individual's house.

Each table had its own theme that reflected the taste and the personality of the woman who later became the hostess of that table. Each hostess provided party favors and arranged for the tea and the sweets for ten people. When you multiply this by ten, you have a hundred people at a memorable tea party.

There were no paper plates, no plastic cups, no signs that we are all too stressed out to live graciously.

The tables were as pretty as the ones of Tiffany fame. Our tea party was a sit-down affair, making it comfortable, civilized, and congenial. Complete strangers were bonded by the desire to live beautifully, and we did, that Saturday afternoon, at that mall. Generosity and kindness abounded, and as a result, no one felt shy. This temporary space was miraculously transformed into a teahouse into which we all walked alone but left filled with a synergy and warmth that remains to this day.

> Friendship renders prosperity more brilliant, while it lightens adversity by sharing and making its burden common.
>
> CICERO

Grateful and fascinated, I asked my friend how she pulled this off. She explained that she had over thirty volunteers, but only ten were actual table hostesses. The others were responsible for decorating the walls with terrific posters, for making the sign THE TEA HOUSE, and for getting everyone energized. It was like a trunk show. Everyone wanted to lend a teapot or silver spoons or a sugar bowl. The days of preparation were fun, she told me. When people love what they're doing, they always talk about the fun, rather than about how hard they worked. Some settings were formal with gleaming silver tea services, others were more casual with odd matching china cups and a mix of china and pottery. But there was

charm in the integrity of each table. Guests walked in and looked about in awe. Several women brought their young daughters along for the experience.

That tea party isn't over. I've heard from several women that as a result of that memorable afternoon, they are still having teas in small groups once a month. Just sitting still, holding a beautiful hand-painted china cup, inhaling the aroma of the herbal infusion or tea leaves, feeling the coziness of the warmth with our fingers, allowing our glasses to fog up as we lean forward in gladness—make us content.

Tea returns us to our center. When we get together in this ritual of renewal and refreshment, we feel a realignment into grace and harmony taking place. You can go to a doctor or a stress manager to learn to slow down, and you can also go to a tea party and learn about wholeness and well-being. Here, there is an added dimension, that of atmosphere, beauty, aesthetics, and art. The smallest moment matters.

Our lives are made up of these micromoments, these openings into truth. What we experience is up to us; all we have to do is accept the invitation to live on a higher level of awareness. When we are awakened, we will enjoy subtle pleasures; we will not need drama in our lives. We will become spiritually attuned and connected to eternity.

A few years ago, friends dropped in. They had driven to New York from Boston. I offered them tea. As I put the kettle on, Jean came into the kitchen to keep me company. I set out the teapot and cups on the tray, and she asked, "Why don't you use the microwave? You can heat the water in ten seconds. At home I have an instant hot-water spout. It's a waste of time to wait for water to boil."

> Zest is the secret of all beauty. There is no beauty that is attractive without zest.
>
> CHRISTIAN DIOR

There are times when you hear something that stuns you. People appear to be rushing to the grave. Grace is banished in the hubbub. I suggested to Jean that she join everyone in the living room and that I'd be right out. Alone, I regained my rhythm. I love the ritual of preparing the tea tray. It does take some time. I like the experience. The process soothes me.

The tea ceremony is the way to serenity, but only if you play by a few rules. You don't heat up water in a microwave. The ritual is all we have.

When we focus on efficiency in our leisure and pleasure time as well as in our business life, we are making a big mistake. The whole idea of tea is to slow down. If you wished to get to the top of the mountain fast, you could get there by helicopter. To be at the summit wouldn't have the same meaning as if you had climbed the mountain one step at a time. The steps we take intensify our reverence for life.

You carry inside you the potential for accomplishment and completeness. You can be in touch with your body and your mind; if we want to, we can all develop a fairly good sense of what's important. Without solitude, and concentration, the spirit is deadened and the mind is numbed.

The secret to the tea party is not to rush. Take the time to feel your breathing, to enjoy the preparations, and to understand that every time you do anything joyfully, grace and serenity will follow.

While other social gatherings might make some people nervous, a tea party should be relaxed. The host or hostess or tea-master is Zen calm. Tea is peaceful. Is it possible that the tea party brings out our truer nature? Do we open ourselves up, let go of conflicts and problems, and experience our lives as part of a larger whole?

The tea party is an opportunity for metamorphosis.

Ontology, the science of metaphysics, teaches us that there is far more to each experience than our limited knowledge and understanding allows us to see.

When participating in a tea ceremony in Japan, you enter through a three-foot-high swinging gate, so low you are forced to bow and be humble. Symbolically, one gives up one's ego. The required waiting station or *machiai* allows guests to make the transition from everyday life into the spiritual dimension of tea. This interlude prepares the guests to appreciate fully the quality of the tea celebration.

> Those who dwell
> among the beauties and
> mysteries of the earth
> are never alone
> or weary of life.
> RACHEL CARSON

The hectic world must be left behind in order to be able to open oneself up to the sacred.

One of my readers from Denver, Colorado, who had spent a few years in England, wrote me that the tea custom had changed his life.

There is an environment of kindness here which I never experience in the States. It is not my work per se, but the way of life which matters so much to me. . . . When I return to the States, I plan to institute chez moi the Sunday afternoon teas of Gertrude Stein's vintage—where it is not the High Tea of British social strata, but the "salon" of the French-Italian Romantic period: a place to cultivate the arts, to talk over ideas. Want to join us?

What an invitation!

At a lecture that Peter was giving at the Dallas Women's Club, I met a charming woman. Right off the bat, Patsie Carver and I carried on as though we were lifelong friends. Several weeks later, I received a chatty letter from her in which she told me about her parents' love affair that had started over tea.

Here it is: Her father, as a young man, had been reluctant to go to a tea party, but his mother insisted that he go. There, at the tea table, his heart leaped, and he fell in love. The marriage was a passionate one, and it stayed that way until his death in old age. When Patsie wrote me her letter, she had no idea I was writing about tea, but how nice to have this wonderful story that illustrates once again the miracles possible over tea. Is this a coincidence, or does this magic elixir excite good fortune and love?

Since I began writing this book, I've become steeped in lore, stories, and information about tea, the equipment, the food that accompanies it, the atmosphere and the ceremonies. A few weeks ago, I went to a friend's "tea champagne" party. The party was from four to seven. The hostess, Barbara Tober, is one of the most accomplished women I know and a very gracious hostess. Her friends are interesting, each one a doer. The energy level was high. Everyone was animated—engaged in conversation. We didn't want the party to end.

Riches and power are but gifts of blind fate, whereas goodness is the result of one's own merits.

HÉLOISE

137

One of Barbara's greatest achievements is her harmonious integration of her life as editor in chief  of *Brides and Your New Home* magazine with a fulfilling private life shared with her husband, Donald. Barbara is elegant, loves pleasure, and is dedicated to excellence. She lives without the breathlessness I see in so many other successful, busy people. I was fascinated by her tea gathering, and so were all her friends.

Barbara's tea for a large group confirmed my belief that tea bags are most practical for parties because everyone can select what they like best. The tea bags look colorful when placed in a basket or plate; I was pleased this arbiter of taste uses tea bags. In a recent *New Yorker,* there was a listing urging the reader to dial the "Bigelow Tea Chest" directly (1-800-841-8158). By simply stocking up on a variety of different types of tea, we can give tea parties easily and have fun while doing it.

Even though all the guests at Barbara's party were working women—some I suspect stay at their offices past seven o'clock most nights—they showed up because the idea was appealing, and sometimes work can just wait. People are making time for tea parties because they value the social exchange that takes place over tea. Now that the eighties are behind us—a time of outdoing, outspending, and overdoing, we are all starved for genuine interaction, honest caring, and the commemoration of meaningful events over the tea ceremony.

Last year, when Peter and I were in Indianapolis, we met an attractive live wire. Bee Young rhapsodized about her love of tea parties. Bee explained that what she liked about tea parties whether they were for family or friends was the fact that she could make all the preparations ahead of time. There are no interruptions, no getting up and going to the kitchen to clear courses. Whether we arrange a tea party at a grand hotel like in the Plaza's Palm Court or at the Ritz in Paris or Claridge's in London; whether we have it in our living room or kitchen, it is nice to have uninterrupted time with our guests.

Better to see the face than to hear the name.

ZEN SAYING

It is a grace note to be on time for a tea party. Many hosts and hostesses do all the work themselves with the help of an older child or friend in the kitchen. Once the tea is prepared, steeped, and ready to be poured, it is bothersome to reheat the water every time a guest arrives. Whether you use tea leaves or tea bags, hot water stays hot only so long.

Not too long ago, I was almost an hour late for a tea in my honor, much to my regret and embarrassment. I was delayed because when I flew into town to lecture, I went to the hall to do a run-through of my slides. To my dismay, I discovered that the huge picture windows in the room made my slides look washed-out. At the last minute, I had to devise silver foil covers for the windows.

The hostess had invited two hundred people to the tea and was waiting by the door when I finally arrived. It was awkward; I apologized.

We all have our excuses for being late, but short of *real* problems, we should try to make every effort to be on time. No one wants to be reminded of how important you are, or how busy you are. We ought to be grateful for having been asked. Far better to decline an invitation gracefully than to go in a rush or accept and then not bother to show up.

Lately, I have sensed that people are tired, discouraged by lack of time, energy, and money. Tea is a notion for the nineties; it is inexpensive and easy to organize. At the same time, there is a certain tenderness attached to it that is not the same as a cocktail party. Tea is usually served by the hostess or host, not a bartender. This personal touch enriches the occasion. The hostess serves, and the friend receives. Each guest's presence is desired, and therefore invitations should be acknowledged promptly. I've never felt warmly toward "regrets only," because the term speaks more of body counts (to know how much you have to pay the caterers) than it does of wanting you to attend and participate in a unique event.

Tea whispers, never shouts. It is a subtle call to lift ourselves above the stresses of the day to a higher level of awareness and appreciation. When we are elevated internally, serenity and peace follow. Tea is an invitation, not a command or an obligation. When you  accept, you are gentled back into your senses. Any life that is too pressured, too frenetic, to take a break and share tea among friends and loved ones is a life off the path.

Chapter VI

TEA

IN THE

GARDEN

Paradise, the word for any idyllic place
where human life began . . . goes back to the
Old Persian for an enclosure or park, just as
the homegrown woods and yard share an
Indo-European root, gher, *meaning some*
kind of domestic enclosure. So it is not
surprising that paradise is invariably
imagined as a garden.

—MAC GRISWOLD

The garden, nature, beauty, and tea. The combination is soothing. Just the thought of this pleasure warms the heart and nourishes the soul. While I love to curl up in a comfortable chair, feet on an ottoman in front of a crackling winter fire, the garden at teatime is still my favorite place on earth to savor the moment and deepen my affection for life.

Tea leaves grow on bushes, nurtured in the good earth by the soil, sun, and rain. In India, whenever you stop at a train station, you can buy tea in a baked clay pot. After you have enjoyed your tea, you may throw the cup out the window. Clay back to clay.

In Persia, the garden means paradise. In the garden, we are rooted, grounded. We take deep breaths, filling ourselves with new life and energy. Tea is not a forbidden fruit; it is an invigorating experience. Though no doctor has ever asked me how often I sip tea in the garden or prescribed it as a cure for my ailments, still I know with certainty that tea has healing properties. Tea puts me in rhythm with nature.

I've always preferred being outside in sunlight to being cooped up indoors. I owe being a decorator to the first garden I tended when I was seven. Gardening is a hands-on experience that engages us with the earth, with the natural flow of things. We are more in touch with nature and therefore with our human nature when we are among flowers, plants, vegetables, and trees. Our cycle is very much in tune with nature's cycle. Every cell in our body is constantly in the process of transformation. The old makes way for the new. Nature

Up above the world you fly; Like a teatray in the sky.
LEWIS CARROLL

creates only to destroy and then create anew. New growth, new chapters, new phases, new seasons. All the cycles of life occur right there in the garden.

The flowers we plant will bloom whether we're there to appreciate them or not. Flowers will die whether we like it or not. And so will we. Our friend the well-known designer Jack Lenor Larsen sug-  gests we never leave home when the garden is in full bloom. Human beings can't live without beauty, and those who don't have access to it die from aesthetic starvation.

Because flowers sustain and strengthen me through the inevitable ups and downs of existence, at difficult times I make myself visualize a garden full of light. I can be at the bedside of a dying family member or friend, and the garden is always there. As I mentioned before, ever since my early childhood, gardens have played an important role in my life.

If you read a great deal of tea lore, you realize that people crave tea because it makes them *feel* better. Placebos work because of the power of suggestion. If you have faith in something, it gives you hope.

Perhaps there is no more sacred place to revere life than in the garden. Not long ago I read a piece in *The New York Times* that explored whether antidepressants help prevent suicide. Because they are so toxic, the article said, an overdose could end up harming the victim more than the depression. Depression, the doctor said, is being unhappy about life experiences. It's simple. If you are *not* unhappy, you are *not* depressed.

I am long on ideas, but short on time. I expect to live only about a hundred years.
THOMAS EDISON

Most people respond to simple, natural beauty. Nature teaches us patience. Look into a gardener's eyes and experience serenity. Look into the face of a tea-master and see light.

When you become a tea-master, you also become a gardener. A famous tea-master once asked an apprentice to sweep the terrace in preparation for the ceremony. Conscientiously, the young Buddhist swept and swept and swept. Every leaf the tree had shed he swept away. Blistered and exhausted, he longed for his master to compliment him on a job well done. Instead, the teacher scolded him, instructing him that beauty is *not* perfection.

Perfection is *not* obtainable. Leaves will continue to fall. A few random leaves are perfectly beautiful. Zen.

At our annual village fair, I bought some intense cobalt-blue delphiniums from a local gardener and put them on a round marble-top table on our tiny terrace. The sun beamed down on these flowers, making each one sparkle, while a tender August breeze rustled the slender stalks and tickled our wind chime. I made a steaming pot of peppermint tea with some sprigs of freshly plucked mint and sat and meditated. I was content. I wanted to enjoy the Persian-blue sky with cumulus cotton-candy clouds, those amazing delphiniums, as the dappled light filtered through the maple trees. That afternoon, our tiny garden became a symbol of all gardens.

I set out an extra cup and saucer in case Peter showed up, though I hadn't invited him. It was a spontaneous moment. I felt that

Do you know that conversation is one of the greatest pleasures in life?

Somerset Maugham

wonderfully satisfying feeling that comes from completing several minor tasks. I'd cleared some weeds, I'd watered the small area, swept the terrace, and, in the spirit of a tea-master, had hosed it as well. I had sprayed the ivy and the low branches of the maple

tree, and they glistened in the sunlight. I felt in perfect harmony with nature, with the season, the time of day, and therefore the cosmos.

As I sat, I watched some of the delphiniums' delicate blue petals fall gently to the tabletop and onto the stone terrace. And I knew not to sweep them away.

Being a tea-master is a subtle art. There is always a tension between the impulse to act and letting nature and the moment speak to us. When we arrange a flower, the flower suggests to us how it will look most graceful. You can't cut the stems by rote or measurement. Flowers talk in the language of beauty, form, and color. They teach us about the preciousness of life. No matter how beautiful they are, they are impermanent. We awaken to them much the way we do to all aspects of our lives. As tea-masters, we can learn to listen with all our senses. Tea in the garden is an unfolding, a surging of spirit. Eventually, I came out of my trance: from a state of harmonious solitude to one of intimate companionship. When Peter came through the door, I looked up. He told me he wished he had a camera because I looked so pretty in the diamond light. When we are serene, our faces change dramatically. We smile from inside, from our garden within.

The tea-master knows it is the subtle, simple, natural beauty that makes the moment sacred. Human souls need to know there is a place to rest, unpressured. I have no idea how long I had been enjoying my tea before Peter joined me. I had experienced a glorious interlude in which I was fully focused on everything around me. Whenever we attain a moment of extraordinary clarity, we have a sense that harmony and deeper meaning exist if we allow it. By being wholly there, I experienced the multiple dimensions of serenity.

Those who are firm, enduring, simple, and unpretentious are the nearest to virtue.
CONFUCIUS

Not until we have learned to respect private moments will we know how to connect with others. We are the same struggling human soul wherever we are, whoever we are with. In our society, so much attention is paid to outward appearances, to signs of wealth, power, and influence. We have devalued the reality of *our* ordinary life's journey. This has impoverished us because we belittle the very things that are the most precious and ultimately the most sacred. It was Thoreau who awakened me to the possibility of inner peace. At Walden Pond, he had three chairs—"Three for society, two for company, and one for solitude." It is in our solitude that we *learn* about living. It is when we look that we *really* see. When we cultivate the minor moments, we become strong. It is this strength that enables us to spread light to others and to celebrate the human condition. I don't think enough of us understand the essential balance between society, company, and solitude. Many of us would do well to have one chair and to sit in it and to pay attention to the person seated.

> That is happiness: to be dissolved into something complete and great.
> WILLA CATHER

People don't always make room for the time necessary to gain inner peace and security. Whenever we are frantic and on overload, scattered and stressed out, we block ourselves from truth and lucidity. Many people find it easier to go to a doctor and get a prescription for tranquilizers. Often, expensive tests are taken, and anger and frustration follow. Energy is depleted. You feel let down and discouraged. You become depressed. We all need to slow down and regain the natural rhythms of our bodies and souls, and allow our minds to clear to make room for our spirits. Tea is a way to this tranquillity.

Just as tea met all of Thoreau's needs, it can meet ours, too. We can start by considering it essential to create private moments in our garden or in a sun-room or a garden room, or wherever we are, for that matter.

In the winter, when the garden is dormant, we can cultivate our inner garden. We can nourish our-selves by paying attention to everything we do and everything we choose not to do. We can read the works of wise and won-derful authors. We can look at plant catalogs and collect seed packages and sip tea and ponder the rhythms of nature and the promise of spring. Listening to the wind, the birds, watching nature bend and flow and yield, takes time and attention.

Tea. Whether we have it alone or with one

> Everything that happens happens as it should, and if you observe carefully, you will find this to be so.
>
> MARCUS AURELIUS

person, or with many, we can go to a garden and experience the mystery, faith, hope, and love that make us serene. Many people feel too busy, too committed, too driven, to take time to be alone, to sip tea quietly and to dream, but this is a missed opportunity. Be there. Experience it yourself. Time is not the enemy. Come, take tea in the garden and see what happens.

This will not be automatic. We must participate. We must be there and sip tea.

After a time of solitude, we instinctively want to connect, share, listen, and relate with another. Tea then becomes a bridge. You and someone you care about come one hundred percent together. The presence of another person now enhances the experience; your energy is not depleted—rather, you are both nourished by the presence of the other. Tea in the garden is soothing, sensuous, calm. Unlike a noisy restaurant, here you can cling to every word, every nuance; in the garden you are private and together. Here you can share silence. There is always a bird singing or a bee buzzing. Tea for two in the garden is intimate. It doesn't matter how old you are. I can remember having tea in 1946 with Mitzi Christian, my godmother, in her garden at Meetinghouse Farm in

> *He did each single thing as if he did nothing else.*
> CHARLES DICKENS

Framingham, Massachusetts. I was five. I also have vivid memories of having tea with Eleanor McMillen Brown in her garden on Long Island the summer of 1963. There were pansies and white radish sandwiches on the tea tray. I also remember tea at the rectory in Wilmington, Delaware, with my grandmother and grandfather when I was seven, the year they both died.

Thoreau tells us that genuine caring is more important than furniture and fixtures. He also suggests that when you shift from solitude to company you do it in the spirit of pulling up an extra chair. You literally put an extra cup and saucer on the tea tray. You are seated; you're close together. Comfort, you discover, is an attitude. When the chemistry is right, you can forget for the moment any aches and pains and experience pure grace.

Tea in the garden is ideal for Thoreau's "society." When you have a tea party outdoors, most often you don't provide seating for everyone. Of course, you can set up round folding tables and have a place for each guest to sit down and eat, but this is not necessary. I've been to many teas where the majority of guests stand. If you have invited a number of older friends, then it is only polite to have some chairs for them to sit on and a table where they can rest their cups and sandwich plates.

Whenever I am in a crowd, I prefer to stand so I'm free to move around and talk to many different people. If I am seated, I often find it hard to break away graciously. When tea in the garden is planned, the weather controls the occasion. Everyone understands this is out of your control. Should the weather

 turn bad, try to visualize how to re-create a garden inside. By using flowered tablecloths and napkins and having lots of flowers around, you can make the experience just as beautiful indoors. The same natural beauty can be, to a large degree, brought inside. Not everyone has a garden, but we can turn our living and dining rooms into garden rooms.

If you have some candelabra, think of using ivy or flowers to decorate them, and do light the candles, even in daylight. The look is very festive.

When planning how much food to prepare, consider six to eight tea sandwiches for each guest. Usually, it is better to serve freshly made sandwiches rather than cookies and cakes. However, people do love to look at a table laden with sweets, and the guests who have a sweet tooth will linger by the table and help themselves. No matter how many guests you have, never use large trays for the sandwiches. It smacks of catering, and trays end up being passed around when there is hardly any food left on them, which is unattractive. I have several dozen small square woven wicker trays with a lip on them, which stack neatly for storage. A white starched luncheon napkin is ideal to place at the bottom. Not only does it catch all the crumbs, but it is elegant. Garnish each tray with parsley sprigs, watercress, flower blossoms, a few radishes, or small tomatoes.

Another attractive alternative to serving tea

Is virtue a thing remote? I wish to be virtuous, and lo! Virtue is at hand.

CONFUCIUS

sandwiches is to cut the top off a loaf of bread, scoop the inside out (much the way you do with pumpkins at Halloween), and fill the bread with tea sandwiches shaped exactly to fit. To avoid waste, the bread you gouge out can be used for stuffing a turkey or bread crumbs. Then take another identical loaf, remove the crust from all four sides, and cut the loaf so that it will fit inside the scooped-out loaf. Now you slice the crustless loaf and make small sandwiches, which you place inside the hollowed-out "bark," fitting them in like a puzzle. The filling for these dainty sandwiches is up to you—egg salad, chopped nuts and cream cheese, ham, etc. Because this presentation is bland in color, place the loaf on a tray with brightly colored flowers. Zinnias or pansies are lively.

When the new minister and his family came to our village, I invited their two daughters over for tea in the garden. Sewell was four and her sister Frances, two. Their mother agreed, Wednesday at five o'clock. Eleanor inquired, "Am I invited, too?" I said of course. Sewell had worn a silver crown in her hair at church the Sunday

> There is no such thing as a sacred idleness.
> GEORGE MACDONALD

before. She wants to be a princess "and a doctor" when she grows up. Children are never too small to be invited to a tea party.

Love and scandal are the best sweeteners of tea.

HENRY FIELDING

We have an artistic gardener in our village. I invited her over for lunch one day. When I apologized for the smallness of our walled garden, she immediately reassured me. "A garden," she said, "is where flowers are." It was the very right thing to say.

But what I discovered that August afternoon with Sewell and Frances is that our small garden area was perfect for them. After both girls had a ride on the old Danish rocking horse in our living room, we went outside, where our tea party would take place. Eleanor had assured me that both girls loved tea. "In South Africa, where we lived until last year, the girls had tea every afternoon. You know, cambric tea. You dip the tea bag in the milk to give it a little flavor." Sewell wanted hot tea, and Frances chose iced tea. While I got their tea ready, the girls played on the grass, licking chocolate-covered ice-cream sticks, nibbling on oatmeal cookies and picking flower petals to make pressed flowers. They tickled the wind chime and explored. By the time I brought out the tea tray, their sundresses were covered with chocolate and vanilla.

He is happiest who hath power to gather wisdom from a flower.
MARY HOWITT

I put a pink glass swizzle in the shape of a candy cane in Frances's glass and a green one for Sewell. I explained to Frances that it was "magic." It was special. She could hold it up in the light and twist the swirls of spun glass and the world would become pink. Fascinated, she played with the magic crystal. Sewell did the same with hers and began to understand what it feels like to be a princess.

Frances told her mommy her tummy was cold. Eleanor held her hot tea glass to her daughter's tummy; the warmth of the glass felt just right. Frances, in all the excitement, gulped her iced tea. Sewell savored hers as she played with her magic wand.

Having finished her tea, Sewell looked down on her sundress, saw the stains, and wanted them to be gone as if by magic. We went to the kitchen sink, which looks directly out onto our tiny patch of grass and garden wall. Whoosh, we squirted some liquid

Clorox 2 on the dress and rubbed. One-two-three, the stains vanished. Before we rejoined the tea party in the garden, Sewell put on one of my bathing suits, a white one with blue and yellow flowers. After tying the back straps together with a ribbon, the princess was ready to make her appearance. We strung some twine across some low branches of the ancient white lilac tree—the very tree that made me fall in love with our old cottage—and hung up the daffodil-yellow sundress with wooden clothespins to dry.

Now Frances wanted to wash her blue dress. The bathing-suit selection was slim pickings, but a red, white, and blue one made do, and after our water play in the sink we hung up another dress next to the wind chimes. On leaving, the girls took home some cookies to their daddy, who had to work and couldn't be with us. Away they went, with ribbons in their hair, dresses in shopping bags, in baggy bathing suits, wet from the hose. Now that's my idea of a *real* tea party in the garden!

When I think of tea in the garden, I think of gorgeous glass pitchers, with sprigs of mint bobbing at the top, and golden orange slices floating in the amber liquid. On a hot summer day, a pitcher of

iced tea on a tray is one of the most refreshing things I can think of. But iced tea is a year-round delight, a pleasant stimulant that is a fine alternative to alcohol. When the temperature rises, and humidity invades the air, ice added to tea is hard to beat.

Pouring hot tea over ice is a relatively recent invention and was discovered right here in America by an Englishman, a tea dealer by the name of Richard Blechynden. In the summer of 1904, he came to St. Louis to the World's Fair to introduce Americans to black tea from India. But in the record-breaking sweltering heat, no one wanted to sample a hot liquid. Out of desperation, he put ice in the glasses, drawing curious people away from the booths selling soda pop and thus giving birth to iced tea. Recent statistics show that approximately eighty percent of all tea in America today is drunk cold or over ice.

When making iced tea, use twice as much tea as you would normally because the ice will dilute the flavor. This is no less economical because as the ice melts there will be that much more tea. I prefer see-through pitchers for iced tea because part of the pleasure is to be able to see the sliced oranges, lemons, and limes. Have fun creating your own flavorful blends. Not only can you use fruits, spices, and herbs, but adding a teaspoon of dark rum to iced tea can transport your spirit to a tropical island.

On a vacation in St. Croix, our hotel packed us a picnic lunch. As soon as we arrived at our secluded beach, we dived into the picnic basket. We immediately discovered that the iced tea had been laced not only with fresh orange juice but also with liberal dashes of Meyers's dark rum! That evening we were told that what we had been given was called "Jamaican iced tea." Any dark rum is good. Try Gosling's Black Seal, a marvelous product of Bermuda.

As I said earlier, I've collected dozens of colorful Venetian blown-glass swizzles for stirring, which I keep in a pitcher on the kitchen counter. I have tall ones for pitchers and shorter ones for glasses. The glass sticks remind some people of the ribbon candy of their childhood. These elegant hand-blown objects are delightful, and make drinking iced tea that much more of a pleasure.

Go to tag sales and have fun finding accessories for iced tea. Last summer we had my dear childhood friend Wendy Defoe and her mother for lunch, and when they were seated at the table, they suddenly remembered my

Experience is not what happens to you; it is what you do with what happens to you.
ALDOUS HUXLEY

mother's silver iced-tea sippers. These look like a silver straw with a tiny spoon at one end and are fun as well as practical. I've added to the few I inherited by scouring antique shops and village fairs. When you're happy buying odd pieces here and there, you can usually get bargains. It's nice to have objects that remind you of the adventure you had in finding them. Secondhand things have a story to tell and are more interesting than things brand-new.

In the 1990s, our society is not as affluent as it used to be, and it feels good to put discarded objects back into service. Recycling is not only an accepted, but a valued practice.

One day, I was browsing at a local village fair. Brooke had found an art-deco desk with a letter rack for six dollars earlier in the day and was home sanding it on the lawn. I spotted a two-tier rectangular tray table. In black crayon, it was marked $8.00. When I handed the woman ten dollars, she gave me back six. "Half price," she said. "It's the end of the fair, and we don't want to have to drag anything back home." My friend Melanie and I walked home with the table, stopping to do some errands along the way. This table is really quite ugly, but I love it and will forever. By putting a cloth over it, I've discovered that the colorful fabric keeps bees away from the food when we're serving tea. Now I have an elegant (four-dollar!) addition to our garden—a tea table.

Tea in the garden. When you have a tea to honor a major life's chapter—a shower before a wedding or birth, a dance for a teenage daughter, a tea to remember an anniversary or birthday—each celebration will be a treasured one. If you want to raise money for a favorite charity or invite friends over to meet an artist, author, or relative, or to show off your garden in bloom, tea in the garden is the best stage setting imaginable. And if you have a yearning to be alone or to have an intimate conversation with one other person, this is an ideal atmosphere of beauty, graciousness, calm, and contentment. In the summer months, we turn our tiny walled-in garden into a living room, where we spend hours reading, writing, visiting with friends, and stopping time by committing ourselves to undisturbed moments where life doesn't race ahead out of control. Nature's beauty seeps into our hearts. Tea in the garden never fails to uplift us, teach us, calm us, and remind us: Life *can* be art. Tea-masters believe it. Tea in the garden proves it.

I hope that by now you're convinced that tea is available to all of us, rich or poor, old or young, sick or healthy. Its benefits are innumerable, and the results of regular tea breaks almost impossible to measure. Like a good book or a trusted friend, tea is one of the simple pleasures that we have lost track of in recent years in our quest for things bigger, better, and faster.

A simple life is its own reward.
GEORGE SANTAYANA

Tea is about slowing down, about reacquainting ourselves with our *selves.* When is the last time you gave your imagination free rein? When was the last time you sat and simply daydreamed? It is these moments of dreaming that bring us in touch, once again, with our earliest goals and fantasies. Remember as a child how hours could fly by when you were just examining a flower or a butterfly? Time can fly again when we immerse ourselves in the moment  and learn to live in the now. Charismatic personalities such as Norman Vincent Peale have proved over and over again the power of dreaming and positive thinking. So indulge yourself. Spend a few minutes and relax over tea doing nothing. Think of it as exercise for your spirit.

Soon, after we have made time for these regular tea breaks, we will feel rejuvenated, refreshed, and ready to share ideas, thoughts, goals, and dreams with the ones we love. After communion with ourselves, we find ourselves ready for communion with others. Socializing, we discover, is not a duty, but a need that comes from the overflow of richness in one's own life, and the desire to share that richness with others. Over tea, socializing becomes an art that delights as well as satisfies.

Whether in the garden, or in a small kitchen, alone, or with a five-year-old child, at Claridge's, or with a group of ten friends, tea is a celebration of a life of the mind *and* senses, a life devoted to the stimulation of beauty.

Who needs to worry about salaries, mortgages, next year's vacation, next week's schedule? Over tea, let yourself be transported to the smoky bazaars of India, or the austere temples of Kyoto. One doesn't need to travel around the world to experience it. Let tea and your imagination be your guide. Spend a few minutes recentering yourself, expanding your horizons, and recapturing tranquillity.

As the end of the twentieth century approaches,

it is more vital than ever before that we learn to treasure ourselves and our planet. We *can* reverse some of the destructive processes of the past. More and more people are becoming in-volved in the movement for ecological awareness.

Tea is a perfect place to begin. Put the kettle on. Make yourself comfortable near a window. Sip, and let the world boil down to just this cup, this moment, and let the warmth slowly spread from your fingers throughout your whole body to your soul. Reflect, analyze, dream, and plan. For now, the world is right here.

Appendix:

A Few Favorite Recipes

Come oh come ye tea-thirsty restless ones—
the kettle boils, bubbles and sings,
musically.

—RABINDRANATH TAGORE

Over my lifetime of tea celebrations, I've been served every imaginable tidbit to go along with tea. Some were sweet, others ranged from salty and fishy to richly buttery. We all have certain traditions, and yet each tea experience is an opportunity to create something different, to combine a variety of ingredients *we* love. Let's be innovative and playful. But remember, you have to like the way your food tastes. If you like it, chances are, so will your friends. If something tastes delicious to you with tea, the nicest compliment you can pay to a friend is to share it.

Always keep in mind that this is *your* tea party. If you have tea alone, you will place on the tray a favorite gingersnap, an orange cookie, or toast with jam. The same rule should be applied when you serve tea to others. If you share tea with a friend, for example, you might ask that friend what kind of tea suits his or her mood. Never ask a guest what he or she would like to eat. It is not gracious, and whatever you've decided on should be prepared in advance of the friend's arrival. An easy rule of thumb to allay your fears of not pleasing your guests' taste buds is to have three different kinds of snacks. No one likes everything; therefore, providing a variety is thoughtful.

Remember, half of all Americans, perhaps more, are overweight. Don't force food. The afternoon tea ceremony is not a substitute for breakfast, lunch, or dinner. We should limit how many times a day we eat, especially foods rich in calories. Peter and I were sent to Singapore by Ambassador Tommy T.B. Koh, then the ambassador to the United Nations, and we were nearly killed with kindness. I'd bought some lightweight cotton skirts for the trip, anticipating the heat and humidity, but after the first week the buttons were popping! Everywhere we went, we were served tea

> Our bodies are our gardens, to which our wills are gardeners.
>
> WILLIAM SHAKESPEARE

with a colorful selection of exotic nibbles, generously passed around throughout the tea party. Some were salty like the fried shrimp crisps, and some were sweet, nutty, crunchy, and rich. But all were tempting, and I couldn't resist the gracious hospitality.

Paradise is where I am.
VOLTAIRE

Eating four or six times a day between meals will have its impact on one's waistline. I've been to many breakfast teas in the South; usually the dining-room table is laden with cakes, muffins, homemade breads, eggs, bacon, sausage, quiche, and cheese and corn puddings. In addition to tea, there are fresh orange juice and champagne mimosas for those who wish them. Even though these parties are called teas, most often there's coffee as well. So though it is called a tea, strictly speaking, it is not one. When Peter and I travel on business, we always have an early breakfast in our room so as to have some time alone to relax, read, and write before our appointments begin. By the time we arrive at an 8:30 "tea," we don't want to eat much, no matter how tempting what is offered might be.

Our good friend John Bowen Coburn, a great man and spiritual leader, once told me, "Grace does not pressure—but offers." Just having food available is a grace note. If someone wants a taste, fine. If not, don't push. As strange as this may sound, I get more pleasure from going to a bakery, looking and smelling, than if I indulge in a sampling of pastries and breads. Taste, we must remember, is only one of our senses. Seeing and smelling can also be satisfying and extremely sensuous. If tea is something we enjoy sharing with others, each of us has to set boundaries on the fattening treats. It should not be considered rude not to eat a hostess's baking.

Now that my children are young adults, living on their own, I've stopped baking. Occasionally, I'll make a batch of blueberry muffins, but only if we have guests, because Peter and I try not to eat a lot of things the main ingredients of which are sugar, butter, and flour. Baking is fun when you have young

children around who can't wait until a batch of Tollhouse cookies or gingersnaps come out hot from the oven. For all of you who love to bake, I'm certain you have made goodies that delighted your family, friends, and guests. Quite apart from the great aroma that spreads all over the house, baking is one of life's great pleasures. I hope you have something in the oven right now.

The wise man becomes full of good, even if he gathers it little by little.

BUDDHA

But for all of you who don't bake, for whatever reason, don't waste a second feeling guilty. Everyone always asks me, "Did you bake the pie, Alexandra?" "Did you bake the Portuguese sweet bread?" "Did you make the chocolate-chip cookies?" "Did you bake the apple tart?" Some people feel that in your own home you should serve only homemade food and desserts. I think this is a fallacy. What enormous pressure we inadvertently put on the host or hostess! Let's put things in perspective: Some of the best restaurants and hotels have independent suppliers who bring in the best bread and pastries daily.

Who cares who made the cookie! Is it delicious? Even famous chefs have someone else making the pastry. Go into any professional kitchen and take a head count. No one does it all. Casting about and trying different specialties from your local bakeries will bring you pleasure and delicious discoveries.

For nearly eight years, I lived on East Sixty-fifth Street between Madison and Fifth avenues above Versailles Patisserie. When Alexandra and Brooke were little, they assumed everyone ate hot croissants fresh from the oven or poppy-seed pastries or flaky, crunchy butterfly pastries every day. The first summer Peter and I were married, we lived on Orange Street in Nantucket, a road famous for the Nantucket Bakery. Every morning at dawn, we'd walk to the bakery, stand in line, and buy our sourdough Portuguese bread for breakfast and for sandwiches to take to the beach.

Freedom simply means the power to carry out your own emotions.

CLARENCE DARROW

Even if many of us did take up baking, chances are we wouldn't be as good as some people for whom baking is a family tradition. It wasn't until recently, for example, that a friend in our village in Connecticut told me the secret to baking Portuguese cookies. I'm including Donna's recipe in this chapter. I paint, but not as well as my favorite artists. I'd rather look at their work than my own. It doesn't make sense to feel under pressure to bake. If you enjoy it and have the time, great. If not, buy some delicious things. That's what money is for. It gives you time. Last summer one of our local chefs in Stonington Village baked some blueberry crumb pies for a luncheon Peter and I were having for friends. The inevitable question came up, "Did you bake this scrumptious pie, Alexandra?" "Stan, a local chef, did. Isn't it great?" As the Häagen-Dazs ice cream melted over the pie, everyone raved about it. The inch-thick crumb topping was so gooey and yummy, we couldn't talk as we savored the flavors and mingling textures.

Let go of the feeling that you have to bake, make your own ice cream, or prepare anything else you serve. If you don't have the urge, go to a store. Recently, an energetic woman bought our local market, which had been closed for nearly a year. Now The  Village Market has all the ingredients for a tea party. Grocery stores sell a whole range of appetizing breads, cookies, biscuits, and treats appropriate for any tea occasion.

In Donna's food market recently, I looked up and down a few aisles for some old familiar favorites like Lorna Doone shortbread cookies and Skippy Creamy peanut butter, which I noted is celebrating its sixtieth-year anniversary. I like Smucker's red raspberry (or strawberry or peach) preserves or Durkee's Marshmallow Fluff or Nabisco Barnum's Animal Crackers. Certain tastes, like old nostalgic smells, recall childhood days, a time when we didn't  count calories but collected butterflies and baseball cards and memories. I can't think of, smell, or taste peanut butter without remembering having cambric tea at the Ritz Carlton in Boston with my mother and godmother, Mitzi Christian, accompanied by triangles of dainty peanut-butter and grape-jelly sandwiches.

Just as designers like us to wear their logo or initials on their fashions, cookie and cracker makers sometimes emboss their name on their product. I often prefer store-bought cookies to ones I buy fresh at a bakery because they are frequently crispier. A good example of this is Swedish gingersnaps. They also keep longer in a canister or airtight tin, whereas a cookie made in a bakery is soon stale.

I am always tempted by Peek Frean Fruit Creme Biscuits and Belgian Butter Almond Cookies. In the early 1950s, Margaret Rudkin searched different countries for delicious cookies she could reproduce in Connecticut. The recipes she found in Belgium resulted in a line of elegant, pretty cookies, delicious enough to tempt any palate. Whether you prefer the chocolate-filled Lido, mint-flavored Milano, Chessman butter cookies, or red-raspberry-puree-filled Chantilly, there is bound to be a cookie to nibble on or dunk in tea that will melt in the mouth and warm the heart. Pepperidge Farm now has a line of Wholesome Choice Cookies that are low in fat.

Tea is a blessing in disguise.

ALEXANDRA STODDARD

Some of the best cookies in the world are baked two villages away from my home in Connecticut. Howard's cookies are extraordinary, and as dangerous to have in the house as a loaded gun. I recommend them to you. Some of my favorites are Chocolate Chunk, Peanut Butter Chocolate Chunk, Alaskan Avalanche made with white chocolate, almonds, and vanilla, Alpine Heaven, made with shortening and almonds, and Orange Almond. I feel Howard is baking just for me. You will, too.

Because most of us don't have seated teas, I prefer cookies to pies. A pie requires a fork; finger food is easier to manage when juggling cup and saucer. If you wish, eliminate the saucer and replace it with a pretty dessert plate that coordinates with the cup. This will leave room for some sandwiches, muffins, and cookies. Everything should be small. If you have a sandwich, cut it into triangles. Small is preferable because it allows people to sample a number of goodies without overdoing it. It's embarrassing to munch on a sandwich dripping tomato-soaked mayonnaise.

Bake or buy small cookies, muffins, scones, biscuits, pastries, tarts, and miniature quiches. To keep sandwiches dainty, remove the crust, whether openfaced or closed. The less chance for crumbs, the better. Avoid crumb cake. Select lemon or orange cake instead, because they can be sliced thinly and cut up into small portions.

Most people associate teas with cucumber sandwiches. I have a weakness for freshly made tea sandwiches. That's another good reason to get to a tea on time, to get there when the wet towel has just been removed from the sandwich tray and everything is just right. I enjoy toast with tea also. In addition to white bread, you can buy thinly sliced dark pumpernickel or seedless rye. Leading bread companies sell whole grain, whole wheat, natural grain, branola, nine grain, crunchy grain, light-style oatmeal wheat, and oatmeal, as well as cinnamon swirl (with or without raisins), apple-walnut bread, and raisin-cinnamon bread. When selecting bread for tea sandwiches, remember it is fun to use a different kind for the top and the bottom. What we serve and eat with our tea is usually not dietetic. However, open any cookbook and study the ingredients of the recipes that tempt you the most. You *can* create healthy options.

> The famous "art of tea" has been deeply impregnated with the spirit of Zen . . . as a "way of spiritual experience."
> THOMAS MERTON

The variety of sandwiches you can concoct with a few basic ingredients at hand and a little imagination is limitless. I taught myself how to make omelettes when I was young by reading *Mastering the Art of French Cooking* by Julia Child. I experimented with a sixty-nine-cent Teflon pan, a dozen eggs, leftovers, and the contents of tin cans from our cupboard. There is an omelette restaurant in New York that lists over a thousand choices on its menu. The least expensive is a plain omelette, and the most costly ones are filled with ingredients like caviar, salmon, and pâté.

Fortunately, my tastes are simple, but I do have a weakness for mâche, the buttery, small-leafed lettuce that is sweet and utterly sublime in a salad or tea sandwiches. Recently, at a fancy gourmet market on Madison Avenue, I picked up some of this treasured green only to find that it cost eighteen dollars a pound! The amount in my bag weighed in at less than six dollars, and I made twenty-four tea sandwiches, so it could have been worse. Keep children in mind when you decide which sandwiches to make, because children should always be welcome unless the hostess is ill or too elderly or simply doesn't like children.

Following is a list of ingredients you may want to have on hand, depending on the season, availability, your whim, and the tea occasion.

For the Tea:

* Sugar
* Honey
* Cinnamon sticks
* Cloves
* Ginger
* Apples
* Pears
* Oranges
* Lemons
* Limes
* Mint sprigs
* Peaches
* Mangoes

For the Sandwiches:

* Salt
* Black and white pepper
* Butter, sweet or salted
* Hellmann's mayonnaise
* Sour cream
* Cream cheese
* Dijon mustard
* Sweet relish
* Sweet pickles
* Olives, green and black
* Peanut butter
* Peach preserves
* Welch's grape jam
* Smucker's strawberry jam
* Marmalade
* Apple jelly
* Raisins
* Walnuts
* Pecans
* Pine nuts
* Almonds
* Cashews
* Cinnamon
* Tomatoes
* Cucumbers

- Dill
- Avocado
- Alfalfa sprouts
- Mâche
- Chives
- Watercress
- Basil
- Chicken
- Eggs
- Ham

My favorite sandwiches smell good and have no fishy odors or strong flavors that may overpower the tea's delicate bouquet. While I adore onions, I don't like  them with tea. An onion sandwich with a glass of red wine on a crisp fall day in New England is heavenly. I love crab, lobster, shrimp, and smoked salmon, but not with tea. I adore caviar and goose-liver pâté, but not with tea. I do not like anchovies; I enjoy capers, but not with tea. I love a whiff of curry powder mixed in with mayonnaise, sour cream, white pepper, and shavings of orange rind. An exotic spice, when properly used, is a pleasant complement to tea, especially the smoky black teas of India and the Sri Lankan mountains.

Many people added salt, not sugar, to their tea early on in its lore. Some like a salty taste more than a sweet one, others prefer a sweet flavor to a salty one. Never be embarrassed about anything you serve if it tastes good to you. If someone bites a corner out of a sandwich that looks mysterious and leaves the rest on the plate, it's all right. Your guests are served these delectable morsels, but they have no obligation to eat something they don't like the taste of any more than you should feel obliged to eat a whole bunch of goodies just because they're there. They won't go to waste. There's always someone who will like what you don't.

The best friends are those who know how to keep the same silences.

BISHOP FULTON J. SHEEN

I prefer cheese and crackers with wine rather than with tea. Salted nuts can be chopped up fine and mixed in with cream cheese and used as a spread, but I'd never serve a dish of nuts with tea. The same applies to cheese sticks. I reserve them for the cocktail hour. But cream cheese and tea are most satisfying companions and soothing to the stomach.

What follows are some recipes for some sweet and savory accompaniments to tea that I particularly like. They were given to me by some wonderful and generous cooks.

I have provided only two sandwich recipes because I have described how I make a few of my favorite ones throughout the text. Armed with mayonnaise, cream cheese, softened butter, and a few other ingredients, you are, I know, very inventive. Just have fun and be blissfully at peace. That is the point.

Lin Shay's Best Lemon Bread

1/2 cup (1 stick) unsalted butter
1 2/3 cups granulated sugar
3 whole eggs
2 1/2 cups unbleached all-purpose flour
1 1/2 tablespoons baking powder
3/4 cup whole milk
Grated rind and juice of one lemon
1 cup chopped pecans
3/4 cup confectioners' sugar

Preheat the oven to 325°F. Butter two 4 1/2- × 8 1/2-inch loaf pans and set aside.

In a large mixing bowl, with an electric mixer, cream the butter with the sugar until light and fluffy. Add the eggs, one at a time, beating well after each addition. Sift together the flour and the baking powder. Stir 2 tablespoons of the lemon juice into the milk. Gradually add the flour and the milk to the butter mixture, alternating ingredients and mixing well after each addition. Fold in the lemon rind and the pecans.

> *Nothing in life is to be feared. It is only to be understood.*
> MARIE CURIE

Pour the batter into the prepared loaf pans and bake in the preheated over for 1 hour, or until a

189

toothpick inserted in the center of the loaves comes out clean.

Mix the remaining lemon juice with the confectioners' sugar and pour over the loaves while they are still hot.

Let the loaves cool in the pans. Lightly coat two sheets of waxed paper or aluminum foil with oil. Unmold the loaves, wrap them tightly in the oiled paper, and set aside for 24 hours.

Serve the loaves thinly sliced.

MAKES TWO 8 1/2-INCH LOAVES

Lin Shay's Moist Apple-Walnut Bread

1/2 cup (1 stick) unsalted butter
3/4 cup granulated sugar
2 large whole eggs
2 large McIntosh apples, peeled and grated
1/2 cup chopped walnuts
1 teaspoon pure vanilla extract
1 3/4 cups unbleached all-purpose flour
1/2 teaspoon salt
1 teaspoon baking soda
1 teaspoon baking powder

Preheat the oven to 350°F. Butter a 4 1/2- ×
8 1/2-inch loaf pan and set aside.

In a large mixing bowl, with an electric mixer,
cream the butter with the sugar until light and fluffy.
Add the eggs, one at a time, beating well after each
addition. Combine the apples with the walnuts and
the vanilla. Fold into the butter mixture and stir well
to combine. Sift together the flour, salt, baking soda,
and baking powder, and gradually add to the wet
ingredients, stirring well to combine.

Pour the batter into the prepared loaf pan and

bake in the preheated oven for 1 hour, or until a toothpick inserted in the center of the loaf comes out clean.

Let the loaf cool in the pan. Unmold and slice to serve.

MAKES ONE 8 1/2-INCH LOAF

Lin Shay's Amaretti

2 2/3 cups blanched almonds
2 cups granulated sugar
1 teaspoon pure almond extract
2 egg whites

Preheat the oven to 350°F. Butter two large baking sheets and set aside.

In a food processor, finely grind the almonds. Combine with 1 cup of the sugar and the almond extract and set aside. In a large mixing bowl, with an electric mixer, beat the egg whites until foamy, then gradually add the second cup of sugar, continuing to beat until stiff. Gently fold the almond mixture into the egg whites.

Using two spoons, shape the dough into 1-inch balls and drop onto the prepared baking sheets, about 1 1/2 inches apart. Bake in the preheated oven for 5 minutes, or until the amaretti are golden.

Let the amaretti cool on the baking sheets for a few minutes, then transfer with a spatula to a wire rack to cool completely.

Stop thinking and start looking.

Thomas Merton

MAKES APPROXIMATELY 2 DOZEN AMARETTI

ALEXANDRA STODDARD

Myra Eisenthal's
Sour Cream Cake

1/2 cup solid shortening
1 cup granulated sugar
2 whole eggs
1 cup sour cream
1 teaspoon pure vanilla extract
2 cups unbleached all-purpose flour
1/2 teaspoon baking soda
1 teaspoon baking powder
1/2 teaspoon salt
1/3 cup brown sugar
1/2 cup chopped walnuts
1 tablespoon ground cinnamon

Preheat the oven to 350°F. Butter a 4 1/2- × 8 1/2-inch loaf pan and set aside.

In a large mixing bowl, with an electric mixer, cream the shortening with the sugar until light and fluffy. Add the eggs, one at a time, beating well after each addition. Stir in the sour cream and the vanilla. Sift together the flour, baking soda, baking powder, and salt. Gradually add to the shortening mixture, beating well to combine. In a small bowl, mix together the brown sugar, walnuts, and cinnamon.

Pour about half the batter into the prepared loaf pan. Top with half the brown sugar mixture. Pour in the remaining batter and top with the rest of the sugar. Bake in the preheated oven for 1 hour, or until a toothpick inserted in the center comes out clean.

Let the loaf cool in the pan. Unmold and slice to serve.

MAKES ONE 8 1/2-INCH LOAF

Donna Duculos's Portuguese Cookies

1 dozen eggs, stored at room temperature overnight
1 teaspoon cream of tartar
1 teaspoon pure vanilla extract
1/2 cup granulated sugar

Preheat the oven to 300°F. Line two large baking sheets with parchment or brown paper (cut-up grocery bags work fine) and set aside.

Separate the eggs, transferring the whites to a large mixing bowl and reserving the yolks for other recipes, such as quiches and crepes. Beat the egg whites until foamy; add the cream of tartar and the vanilla and mix well. Gradually add the sugar, continuing to beat until stiff.

Using two teaspoons, drop rounds of meringue onto the prepared baking sheets, about 1 1/2 inches apart. Lower the oven temperature to 275°F. and bake for 1 1/2 hours, or until the cookies are firm. Let the cookies cool on the baking sheets for a few minutes, then transfer with a spatula to a wire rack to cool completely. Continue baking the cookies in batches until all the meringue has been used.

MAKES APPROXIMATELY 5 DOZEN 1-INCH COOKIES

Charlie Palmer and Aureole's
Toasted Almond and Raspberry Savories

1/2 cup (1 stick) unsalted butter
1 cup granulated sugar
1/2 cup egg whites (from approximately 3 eggs)
2 cups unbleached all-purpose flour
1 1/4 tablespoons baking powder
1/2 teaspoon salt
1 tablespoon ground cinnamon
1 cup whole milk
2 standard containers of fresh raspberries
1/2 cup sliced almonds

Preheat the oven to 350°F. Butter twelve 2-inch muffin tins or brioche molds and set aside.

In a large mixing bowl, with an electric mixer, cream the butter with the sugar until light and fluffy. Gradually add the egg whites, continuing to beat until well combined. Sift together the flour, baking powder, salt, and cinnamon, and add to the butter mixture, along with the milk. Stir together just to incorporate and obtain a smooth batter; do not overmix.

Place about 1 tablespoon of batter in each of the

Act without doing; work without effort.
TAO-TE CHING

197

prepared tins. Add four or five raspberries to each. Cover with enough batter to fill the tins three-quarters full. Top with four or five more raspberries and a sprinkling of almonds.

Place in the preheated oven and bake for 15 minutes, or until the savories are golden brown and firm to the touch. Let cool in the pan for a few minutes, then invert onto a wire rack and serve immediately, while still warm.

MAKES 1 DOZEN SAVORIES

Deborah Jensen's Buttermilk Scones

5 cups unbleached all-purpose flour
1 cup granulated sugar
1 teaspoon salt
2 tablespoons plus 1/2 teaspoon baking powder
2 teaspoons baking soda
2 tablespoons solid shortening
1/2 cup unsalted butter
2 whole eggs
1 1/2 cups buttermilk
1 1/2 cups raisins, currants, or blueberries
1 egg white

Preheat the oven to 450°F.

In a large mixing bowl, sift together the dry ingredients. With your fingers, gently rub the shortening and butter into the flour mixture. The mixture should look like soft bread crumbs or wet sand. Add the whole eggs, one at a time, and then the buttermilk, mixing well after each addition. Dust the raisins with flour and add to the dough. Knead the dough fifteen turns, then turn out onto a well-floured surface and, with your hands, form into a square approximately 10 inches × 10 inches and 2 inches thick. With an unserrated knife, cut the dough into twenty-four small squares. Quickly place them on two large baking sheets, about 2 inches apart, and brush with the egg white.

Place in the preheated oven and bake for 20 minutes, or until the scones just begin to brown but do not lose their square shape. Let the scones cool on the baking sheets for a few minutes, then transfer to a serving plate and serve warm.

MAKES 2 DOZEN TEA SCONES

Deborah Jensen's Berry Muffins

2 whole eggs, beaten
1/2 cup whole milk
1/4 cup (1/2 stick) unsalted butter, melted
2 cups unbleached all-purpose flour
1 tablespoon baking powder
1/2 teaspoon salt
1/2 cup granulated sugar
1 cup blueberries, raspberries, or other berries

Preheat the oven to 400°F. Line twenty-four 2-inch muffin tins with paper cupcake holders and set aside.

In a large mixing bowl, with an electric mixer, beat the eggs until foamy. Stir in the milk and the butter. Sift the flour with the baking powder, salt, and sugar. Fold into the wet ingredients, stirring just to incorporate; do not overmix. Gently fold the berries into the batter.

Pour the batter into the prepared muffin tins and bake in the preheated oven for 12 minutes, or

> *We shape clay into a pot, but it is the emptiness inside that holds whatever we want.*
> Tao-te Ching

until the muffins are lightly browned and firm to the touch. Let cool in the pan for a few minutes, then invert onto a wire rack and serve immediately, while still warm.

MAKES 2 DOZEN TEA MUFFINS

Rita Hall's Shortbread

1/2 cup (1 stick) lightly salted butter
1/4 cup granulated sugar
3/4 cup unbleached all-purpose flour
1/4 cup cornstarch

Preheat the oven to 350°F. Line a large baking sheet with parchment and set aside.

In a large mixing bowl, with an electric mixer, cream the butter. Slowly add the sugar, continuing to beat until the mixture is a pale lemon color. Sift the flour with the cornstarch and add to the butter mixture, a tablespoon at a time, stirring well to combine.

Turn the dough out onto a lightly floured surface and, with a rolling pin, roll into an 8-inch, 1/4-inch-thick circle. Gently prick with a fork, and sprinkle lightly with sugar. Lay the dough on the prepared baking sheet and refrigerate for fifteen minutes.

Place in the preheated oven and bake for 30 minutes, or until the shortbread is lightly browned. Let cool on the baking sheet for a few minutes, then cut into wedges and serve immediately, while still warm.

MAKES 8 WEDGES OF SHORTBREAD

Suzanne Guerlain's Chocolate Truffles

3/4 cup (1 1/2 sticks) unsalted butter
2 cups granulated sugar
4 ounces unsweetened chocolate, melted
4 whole eggs
1 cup unbleached all-purpose flour
1/2 teaspoon salt
1 teaspoon pure vanilla extract
1/4 cup heavy cream, approximately
Kahlúa to taste
Confectioners' sugar

Preheat the oven to 350°F. Butter an 8-inch square baking pan and set aside.

In a large bowl, with an electric mixer, or in a food processor, cream together the butter and sugar until light and fluffy. Add the chocolate and beat to combine. Blend in the eggs, one at a time, then add the flour, salt, and vanilla, and mix well.

Pour the batter into the prepared baking pan and bake in the preheated oven for 20 minutes, or until a toothpick inserted in the center comes out clean. The brownie should be quite moist. Set aside to cool in the pan.

When the brownie is completely cool, remove

from the pan and crumble into a large bowl. Add the heavy cream and Kahlúa, just enough of each to make the brownie crumbs into a firm dough that you can roll into 1-inch balls. Place the balls in a single layer on a platter and refrigerate.

Shortly before serving, remove the balls from the refrigerator and gently roll in confectioners' sugar. (It is best to take the balls out of the refrigerator no more than 1 hour before serving. If the truffles are rolled in the confectioners' sugar too far in advance, they will absorb the sugar and will not look fresh.) Set the truffles in tiny paper holders and place on a decorative plate to serve.

MAKES APPROXIMATELY 3 DOZEN 1-INCH TRUFFLES

VARIATIONS:

1. Use 1 tablespoon almond extract in place of the vanilla and roll the chilled balls in chopped almonds.

2. Use approximately 3 tablespoons raspberry liqueur in place of the Kahlúa and roll the chilled balls in miniature chocolate chips.

Thelma's Sour Cream Pound Cake

1 cup (2 sticks) unsalted butter or margarine
3 cups granulated sugar
6 whole eggs
1 cup sour cream
3 cups unbleached all-purpose flour
1/4 teaspoon baking soda
1 teaspoon pure vanilla extract

Preheat the oven to 325°F. Butter a 10-inch tube pan, dust with flour, and set aside.

In a large mixing bowl, with an electric mixer, cream the butter, then gradually add the sugar, continuing to beat until light and fluffy. Add the eggs, one at a time, beating well after each addition. Stir in the sour cream. Sift the flour with the baking soda, and then sift the mixture again. Add to the wet ingredients, 1/2 cup at a time, beating well after each addition. Add the vanilla and mix well.

Pour the batter into the prepared pan and bake in the preheated oven for 1 1/2 hours, or until a toothpick inserted in the center of the cake comes out clean. Let the cake cool in the pan on a wire rack for 5 minutes. Run a spatula or the dull side of a knife around the edge of the pan to loosen the cake and turn out onto the rack to cool completely.

Cut into slices and serve plain.

MAKES ONE 10-INCH CAKE

VARIATION:

Use 1 teaspoon lemon extract or 1/2 teaspoon almond extract in place of the vanilla.

ALEXANDRA STODDARD

Miss Quinnell's Pound Cake

1 1/2 cups (3 sticks) unsalted butter
2 1/2 cups granulated sugar
7 whole eggs
1 egg yolk
3 cups cake flour
1/2 teaspoon salt
1 teaspoon pure vanilla extract

Preheat the oven to 300°F. Butter a 9-inch loaf pan, dust with flour, and set aside.

In a large mixing bowl, with an electric mixer, cream the butter, then gradually add the sugar, continuing to beat until light and fluffy. Add the eggs and the egg yolk, one at a time, beating well after each addition. Sift together the flour and the salt, measure out 3 cups of the flour mixture, and add to the butter mixture along with the vanilla. Beat well to combine.

Pour the batter into the prepared pan and bake in the preheated oven for 1 hour and 50 minutes,

> To go against the dominant thinking of your friends, of most of the people you see every day, is perhaps the most difficult act of heroism you can perform.
> THEODORE H. WHITE

or until a toothpick inserted in the center comes out clean. Let cool in the pan on a wire rack for a few minutes. Run a spatula or the dull side of a knife around the edges of the pan to loosen the cake and turn out onto the rack to cool completely.

Serve the loaf thinly sliced.

MAKES ONE 9-INCH LOAF

Mary Ann Petro's Celebration Cookies

1 cup melted margarine
1 cup granulated sugar
1 cup light brown sugar
2 whole eggs
1 teaspoon pure vanilla extract
2 cups unbleached all-purpose flour
1 teaspoon baking soda
1 cup old-fashioned oatmeal
1 cup cornflakes, crushed
3 ounces chocolate chips
1/2 cup chopped pecans or walnuts

Preheat the oven to 350°F. Butter two large baking sheets and set aside.

In a large mixing bowl, with an electric mixer, beat the margarine with the white and brown sugars until well combined. Add the eggs, one at a time, mixing well after each addition. Stir in the vanilla. Sift together the flour, baking soda, and baking powder, and gradually add to the wet ingredients, beating well after each addition. Fold in the oatmeal, cornflakes, chocolate chips, and walnuts, and stir well to combine.

Drop the dough, a teaspoon at a time, onto the prepared baking sheets, about 2 inches apart. Bake in the preheated oven for 12 minutes, or until the cookies are lightly browned. Let cool on the baking sheets for a few minutes, then transfer with a spatula to a wire rack to cool completely.

MAKES APPROXIMATELY 2 DOZEN
1 1/2-INCH COOKIES

Mary Ann Petro's Watercress and Egg Tea Sandwiches

6 hard-boiled eggs, peeled and mashed
2 bunches of watercress, washed, stems removed, and
  coarsely chopped
1/4 cup chopped fresh chives
1/2 cup (approximately) homemade or fine-quality
  mayonnaise
Salt and pepper to taste
Tabasco sauce to taste
Fresh pumpernickel, sourdough, or whole-wheat bread,
  sliced
1/4 cup chopped fresh parsley
Additional watercress and chives, plus green olives for
  garnish, optional

In a mixing bowl, combine the eggs, chopped watercress, and chopped chives with just enough mayonnaise to moisten and bind the mixture. Season with salt and pepper and Tabasco and mix well.

Using one or several kinds of bread, cut the slices into interesting shapes, using whatever cookie cutters you have on hand. Spread the egg and watercress mixture onto half the bread shapes and top each with a matching shape. Lightly spread the outside edge of each sandwich with mayonnaise, roll in the parsley, and serve on a bed of additional watercress and chives, garnished with green olives, if desired. Decorate with fresh blossoms (pansies are nice).

MAKES 2 DOZEN TO 3 DOZEN

TEA SANDWICHES

Mary Ann Petro's Toasted Pecan Tea Sandwiches

2 teaspoons melted butter
Worcestershire sauce
Tabasco sauce
Salt to taste
2 cups pecan halves
8 ounces cream cheese
Garlic salt
Cayenne pepper
Fresh white bread, thinly sliced

Preheat the oven to 300°F.

In a mixing bowl, combine the butter with 3 tablespoons of Worcestershire, 3 dashes of Tabasco, and the salt. Add the pecans, stir to coat thoroughly, and set aside to marinate for 5 minutes.

Drain the pecans, spread in a single layer on a large baking sheet, and toast in the preheated oven for 15 minutes, or until dry. Chop the pecans and set aside.

In another mixing bowl, blend the cream cheese with Worcestershire, Tabasco, garlic salt, and cayenne

Truth is something that works. It is a vehicle empowered to carry us to our destination.
JOYCE CAROL OATES

214

to taste. (Do not overseason at this point, as the pecans are already spicy.) Stir in the chopped pecans. Taste the mixture and adjust the seasonings if necessary.

Trim the crusts from the bread slices. Cut each slice diagonally into two triangles. Spread a thin layer of cream cheese on one triangle, top with the other half, and transfer to a platter to serve.

MAKES APPROXIMATELY 2 DOZEN

TEA SANDWICHES

Mary Ann Petro's Swan Kisses

3 egg whites
1 cup brown sugar
1 teaspoon pure vanilla extract
1 teaspoon strong good-quality brewed coffee
1 cup hazelnuts, blanched, toasted, and ground
1 pint fresh raspberries
1 pint heavy cream, whipped
Fresh mint for garnish

Preheat the oven to 250°F. Butter two large baking sheets and set aside.

In a large mixing bowl, with an electric mixer, beat the egg whites until foamy, then gradually add the sugar, continuing to beat until stiff. Fold in the vanilla, the coffee, and the hazelnuts, and beat again until stiff.

Using two teaspoons, shape the batter into rounds and drop onto the prepared baking sheets, about 1 inch apart. Bake in the preheated oven for 1 hour, or until the kisses are dry to the touch. Let the kisses cool on the baking sheets for a few minutes, then transfer with a spatula to a wire rack to cool completely.

To serve, place a few kisses on a small dessert plate. Spoon some raspberries and whipped cream alongside, and garnish with a sprig of mint.

MAKES APPROXIMATELY 3 DOZEN

1 1/2-INCH KISSES

Mary Ann Petro's Tiny Pecan Pies

3 ounces cream cheese
1/2 cup (1 stick) plus 1 tablespoon unsalted butter, softened
1 cup sifted unbleached all-purpose flour
1 whole egg
3/4 cup brown sugar
1 teaspoon pure vanilla extract
Pinch of salt
2/3 cup chopped pecans

Preheat the oven to 325°F.

In a large mixing bowl, with an electric mixer, blend the cream cheese and the 1/2 cup butter. Gradually add the flour, beating well after each addition. Divide the dough into twenty-four 1-inch balls and press into the bottom and up the sides of twenty-four ungreased 2-inch muffin tins.

In a clean bowl, with the electric mixer, beat the egg until foamy, then gradually add the brown sugar, the remaining 1 tablespoon butter, the vanilla, and salt, beating well after each addition.

Sprinkle half of the pecans into the pastry-lined muffin tins. Divide the egg filling evenly among the tins, and sprinkle the remaining pecans over the top of the filling. Bake in the preheated oven for 25 minutes, or until the pastry is golden and the filling is firm. Let the pies cool completely in the tins, then transfer to a platter to serve.

MAKES TWENTY-FOUR 2-INCH PIES

Deborah Jensen's
Raspberry-Almond Bars

3/4 cup (1 1/2 sticks) unsalted butter, softened
1/4 cup granulated sugar
1/2 cup brown sugar
2 egg yolks
1 teaspoon pure vanilla extract
2 cups unbleached all-purpose flour
1 teaspoon baking powder
1/2 teaspoon baking soda
1/2 teaspoon salt
1 cup chopped almonds
2 tablespoons freshly squeezed lemon juice
2/3 cup raspberry jam (or another flavor, if preferred)
Confectioners' sugar

Preheat the oven to 325°F. Butter a 9-inch square or an 11- × 7- × 2-inch rectangular baking pan, dust with flour, and set aside.

In a large mixing bowl, with an electric mixer, cream the butter with the white and brown sugars until light and fluffy. Add the egg yolks, one at a time, and the vanilla, beating well after each addition. Sift together the flour, baking powder, baking soda, and salt, and add to the wet ingredients, stirring just to incorporate; do not overmix. Reserve 3 tablespoons of the almonds for topping; fold the remainder into the dough.

In a small bowl, combine the lemon juice with the jam and mix well.

Press half of the dough into the bottom of the prepared pan. Lightly spread the jam mixture over the dough, then crumble the remaining dough on top of the jam. Sprinkle with the reserved almonds. Bake in the preheated oven for 1 hour, or until the pastry is golden and the filling is firm. Let cool completely in the pan, then cut into bite-size pieces, dust with confectioners' sugar, and transfer to a platter to serve.

MAKES 3 DOZEN 1 1/2-INCH BARS

Suzanne Guerlain's Tiny Chicken Waldorf Cream Puffs

For the puffs:
1 cup water
1/2 cup unsalted butter or margarine
1 cup unbleached all-purpose flour
4 whole eggs

For the filling:
2 whole boneless chicken breasts
1/4 cup chopped walnuts
1/4 cup raisins
1 teaspoon freshly squeezed lemon juice
1/2 cup good-quality mayonnaise
1/4 teaspoon celery seed
Salt and pepper to taste

Preheat the oven to 400°F. Butter two large baking sheets and set aside.

In the top of a double boiler, over boiling water, combine the water and the butter and bring to a simmer. Add the flour and then the eggs, one at a time, stirring vigorously and constantly to form a thick, very smooth mixture that pulls away from the sides of the pan.

Transfer the mixture to a pastry bag and pipe, a tablespoon at a time, about 2 inches apart, onto the prepared baking sheets. Bake in the preheated oven for 20 minutes, or until the pastries are well browned. Let cool on the baking sheet for a few minutes, then transfer with a spatula to a wire rack to cool completely. Store the cooled puffs in a covered container until ready to use.

Microwave the chicken breasts until the meat is fully cooked but still moist (or use any other cooking method you prefer). In a food processor, coarsely chop the chicken. Transfer to a mixing bowl, add the remaining ingredients, and mix well. Cover and refrigerate overnight.

Split the pastry puffs in half horizontally, and hollow out each half by removing the moist center section. No more than 2 hours before serving, spoon a generous portion of the chicken mixture into the bottom half of each pastry puff and replace the top of the puff. Place the filled puffs on a platter and refrigerate until ready to serve.

MAKES APPROXIMATELY
EIGHTEEN 2-INCH PUFFS

Acknowledgment
with appreciation

Carl Brandt
As always, I want to thank my literary agent and friend, who makes everything possible.

Rose Marie Morse
My editor, who suggested I put my love of tea on paper, thank you for polishing this tea celebration, sipping, tasting, and testing recipes. You are a tea-master of great intelligence and beauty.

Steve Freeburg
Your love of tea and your illustrations are inspiring. Thank you.

Marysarah Quinn
What fun we've had sipping herbal tea and designing our ninth book together. Thanks, babe.

Brooke Stoddard
The photograph you styled for the cover is breathtaking. I'm proud of you. Love and thanks.

Elisabeth Carey Lewis
Thank you for your help, encouragement, dedication, and belief in our mission.

Russell Gordon
I love working with you on my book jackets because you understand and care. Thanks for your talent and enthusiasm.

Sarah Zimmerman
Thank you for your typing, but that is the least of it. It is for your caring wisdom that I come to you and am always enriched.

Friends
Thank you for your recipes, which enhance the pleasures of the tea celebration. I appreciate your talent and our friendship.

My readers
You awaken me to my senses. Thank you for sending me tea bags in your letters, for having me over for tea when I'm in your hometown, and for reminding me how often you sip tea with a deep sense of serenity.